EXCURSIONS FROM
PEAK TO PEAK
THEN AND NOW

by Silvia Pettem

© 1997
Tourism and Recreation Program
of Boulder County, Inc. (TARP)
Boulder Chamber of Commerce
2440 Pearl Street, Boulder CO 80302

Funding provided by the Colorado Historical Society.

All rights reserved.

Peak to Peak Series #1
ISBN 0-9617799-9-3

The cover photo shows a section of the Peak to Peak Highway near Ward, with Mount Audubon in the distance. Photo by L. C. McClure. Carnegie Branch Library for Local History, Boulder Historical Society Collection.

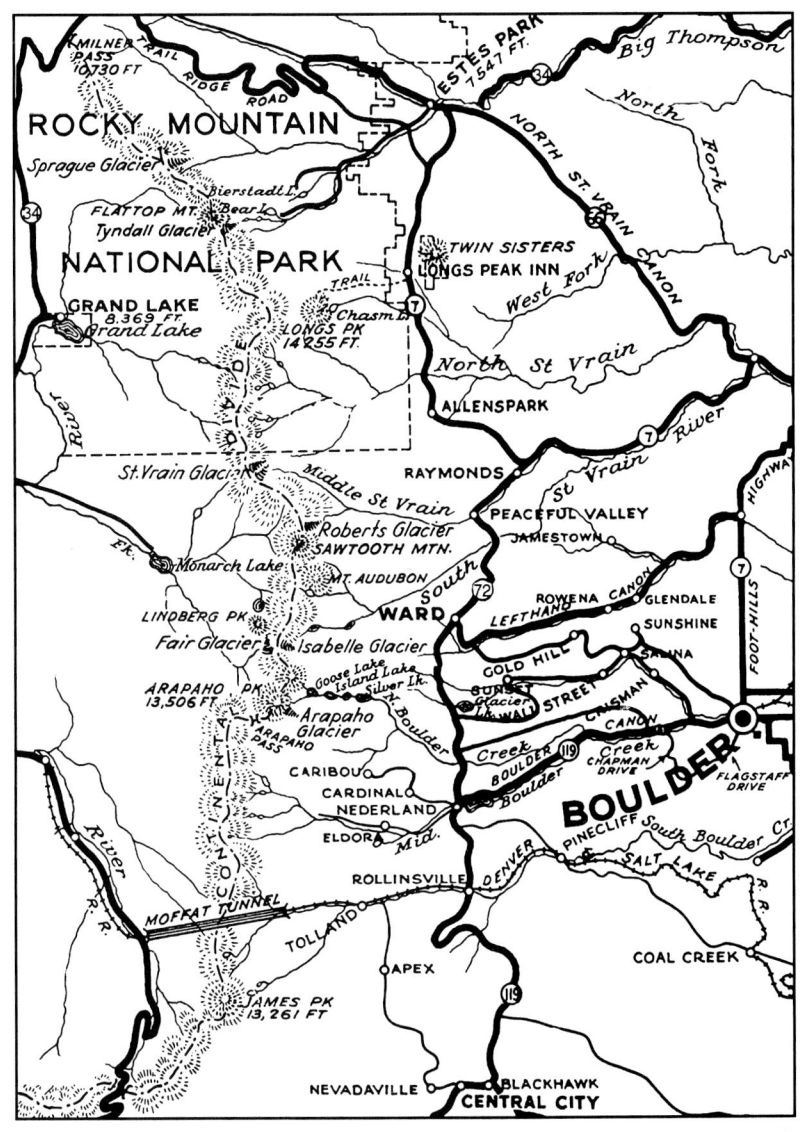

This map of the Peak to Peak Region is based on a Boulder Chamber of Commerce map from 1946. Pettem collection.

To Ed, Daisy, Sean, and Clara.

With special thanks to Scott Bruntjen, Jody Corruccini, Wendy Hall, Tom Meier, and Mary Jo Reitsema.

CONTENTS

PART I
TOURISM ALONG THE PEAK TO PEAK HIGHWAY --

Introduction	1
Miners Built the Roads, Black Hawk to Ward	3
Railroads Brought the Early Tourists	9
The Age of the Automobile, Ward to Estes Park	13
Scenery (and Good Roads) Made Them Stay	19
Gateway to the Glaciers	25
Tourism Continues	33

PART II
THE PEAK TO PEAK, A GUIDED TOUR --

Black Hawk and Central City	37
Rollinsville and the Moffat Road	41
Eldora, Sulphide Flats, and the Lake Eldora Area	47
Nederland	55
Caribou	61
The Switzerland Trail	65
Gold Hill	73
Ward	79
Brainard Lake and Peaceful Valley	87
Allenspark Area	93
Estes Park	101

PART III
BOULDER LOOP TOUR --

Peak to Peak Highway, South Saint Vrain Canyon, Lyons, Boulder, and Boulder Canyon	105

FURTHER READING	120
INDEX	124

These early Peak to Peak area tourists posed for J. B. Sturtevant after a day in the mountains picking wild flowers. Photo dated August 27, 1904. Carnegie Branch Library for Local History, Boulder Historical Society Collection.

INTRODUCTION

The Peak to Peak Highway runs from Clear Creek Canyon, through Black Hawk, Rollinsville, Nederland and Ward, then north to Peaceful Valley, Allenspark and, finally, Estes Park, the gateway to Rocky Mountain National Park. The highway crosses Gilpin, Boulder, and Larimer Counties as it winds its way for over sixty miles of outstanding mountain scenery.

The first section of this book will follow the growth of tourism from the mining and railroading days through the age of the automobile, and discuss scenic attractions and improvements along the Peak to Peak Highway.

The second section will guide you from the Black Hawk/Central City area to Estes Park. Included are numerous side trips to historic mining and resort towns such as Eldora and Gold Hill, the railroad grades of the Moffat Road and the Switzerland Trail, and to Red Rock and Brainard Lakes where you'll see spectacular vistas of the Indian Peak Wilderness.

A loop tour through Lyons and Boulder makes up the final section and is included for those with more time or for visitors who want to experience the diversity of the mountains and plains.

The Peak to Peak Highway has three different route numbers. If you drive north from Central City and Black Hawk, you'll be on Colorado 119. After crossing South Beaver Creek,

Colorado 72 joins the Highway, and the two run north jointly to Nederland. From there, Colorado 119 follows Boulder Canyon to Boulder while Colorado 72 continues north from Nederland past Ward and Peaceful Valley. A few miles north of Peaceful Valley, Colorado 72 intersects Colorado 7 between Lyons and Allenspark. The final portion of the Highway follows Colorado 7 as it continues on to Allenspark and Estes Park.

Most of the sites covered in this book can be seen from your car on public roadways. Others such as a close-up view of Arapaho [also spelled Arapahoe] Glacier require a hike on public trails. When on a hike, leave the area as you would like to find it, and pack out what you pack in. Please resist the urge to trespass on private property. Many historic mining sites are dangerous, and individuals living in the Peak to Peak area appreciate the privacy of their homes.

To reach the Peak to Peak Highway -

From U.S. 6 in Clear Creek Canyon, turn north onto Colorado 119 towards Black Hawk and Rollinsville.

From Estes Park turn south on Colorado 7 towards Meeker Park and Allenspark.

From Boulder go west on Colorado 119 towards Nederland. From Lyons go west on Colorado 7 towards Allenspark.

The Boulder Loop tour covers Colorado 72 on the Peak to Peak Highway, Colorado 7 in South St. Vrain Canyon, U.S. 36 between Lyons and Boulder, and Colorado 119 in Boulder Canyon. For the latest maps and tourist information, stop at the visitors' centers in Nederland and Lyons.

PART I

MINERS BUILT THE ROADS
(BLACK HAWK TO WARD)

Arapahoes on the plains and Utes in the mountains lived quietly for many years in what is now north-central Colorado. Suddenly, prospectors found "color" near present-day Denver, and the peaceful landscape never was the same. Out-of-work easterners had gold fever and joined the "Pikes Peak gold rush," so named because even though no gold would be found near Pikes Peak for many years, the mountain was the only well-known landmark in the central Rocky Mountains.

As the gold-seekers neared the mountains on their westward travels, a few of the men broke off from the others and followed Boulder Creek to the mouth of Boulder Canyon (then spelled Canon). The prospectors built crude cabins, then panned the gravels of Boulder Creek. After they found some nuggets and flakes, they decided to look for the source of the gold higher up in the foothills. There was little snow that year, so some of the men followed an old Indian trail up the ridge between Left Hand and Four Mile Creeks, west of present-day Boulder. In January, 1859, they found what they had been looking for --- a sizable deposit of gold in a creek they named Gold Run. Their camp became Gold Hill.

When discouraged prospectors in the Denver area heard the news, they rushed to the new mining camp. Around the same time, George Jackson found gold on Chicago Creek near Idaho Springs, and John Gregory found gold between present-day Black Hawk and Central City.

That summer, all three areas became bustling gold mining camps. The Central City district was called "the richest square mile on earth." Gold ore from the mines in and around Central City was hauled to Black Hawk for processing in the mills that drew water from North Clear Creek. In Boulder County, gold was mined in Gold Hill and, farther north, in Ward. Some of the ore from these towns was transported, at first on burros and later by wagons, to the Black Hawk gold mills.

The earliest mountain roads followed animal and Indian trails. By 1864, the "road" between Ward and Black Hawk was improved as the Niwot and Black Hawk Wagon Road. It started at the mouth of Left Hand Canyon, went up to Ward, then extended from Ward south to include the mining camp of Sunnyside, as well as Hill's Ranch (Caribou Ranch), Brown's Crossing (Nederland), and Rollinsville. By 1872 the road along this same route also accessed Puzzler, Sherwood Gulch, and the Washington Avenue mine which was at the head of Pennsylvania Gulch.

Although the search for gold brought the first settlers, and the first roads, a silver strike in Caribou, in 1869, turned the ranching community of what is now Nederland into a major transportation center. The Boulder Canyon road, under construction when the silver boom began, was completed in 1871 as a one-lane dirt road through the town. Supplies from Boulder were hauled directly to Caribou, west of Nederland

and, at 10,000 feet, close to the Continental Divide. The Boulder-Caribou and the Ward-Black Hawk roads intersected at Nederland, just as they do today.

Prospectors had studio portraits taken in order to show their families back home that they were part of the gold rush. Photo by J. B. Sturtevant. Pettem collection.

In 1872, the discovery of gold in combination with tellurium brought about a second gold rush. Many new mining camps, including Sunshine, Wallstreet, and Salina grew up among a network of hastily-constructed wagon roads. Prospectors who didn't strike it rich still were able to find steady work as laborers in the mines. These miners sent for their families and built churches and schools which created permanent communities. Just after the first building of the Salina school opened in 1875 one newspaper stated, "There are not many children in Salina, but if the citizens are diligent, I think we will be able to keep the school marm busy before a great while."

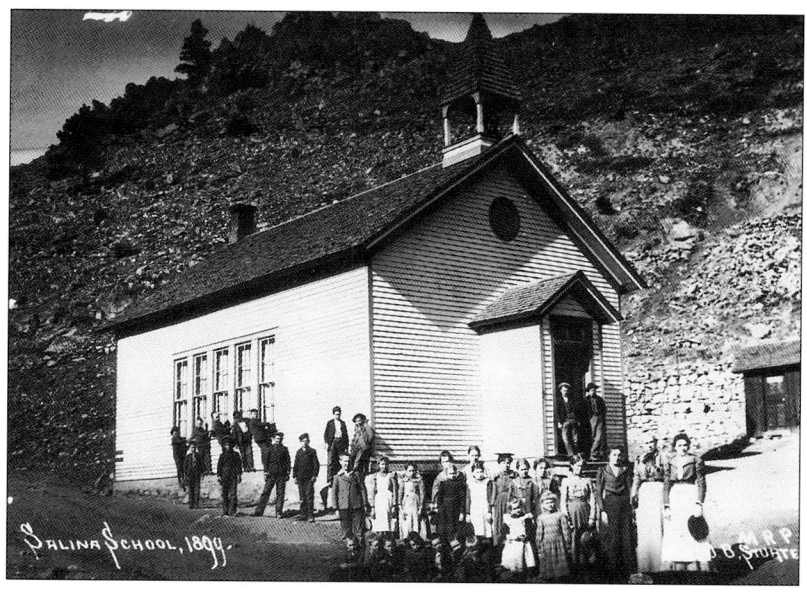

Miners brought their families and settled permanent communities. This second Salina School was built in 1885. Although no longer used for classes, the building is still in use by the community. Photo by J. B. Sturtevant. Carnegie Branch Library for Local History, Boulder Historical Society Collection.

The Little Church in the Pines was built in 1908. Photo by author, 1980.

After the Greeley, Salt Lake & Pacific Railroad reached Sunset, the Colorado & Northwestern built a branch north to Ward. Soon the railroad became known as the Switzerland Trail of America. Rick Sinner collection.

RAILROADS BROUGHT THE EARLY TOURISTS

Railroads soon followed the wagon roads. The narrow gauge (three feet between the rails) Greeley, Salt Lake & Pacific, which never saw its namesakes, was built in 1883 to serve the Boulder County gold mining towns. The railroad extended from Boulder, up Four Mile Canyon, to what is now Sunset, with wagon road connections to Gold Hill and Ward. In 1898, the railroad was continued north to Ward under the new ownership of the Colorado and Northwestern. A second branch wound its way south to Eldora in 1905.

Although the purpose of the railroad was to haul in coal for steam-powered mining equipment and bring out ore, trains soon became popular with tourists. The enthusiasm of the "flatlanders" knew no bounds. A whole new world opened up to people from the plains when the "Switzerland Trail of America," as the railroad was called, reached its final destinations.

Summer snowball excursions, "almost to the realm of perpetual snow," lured city dwellers to Ward. The Eldora line advertised "wild flower excursions." The train made numerous stops for passengers to "dismount and gather great bouquets of rare beauty." (Colorado law now prohibits the picking of columbines, the state flower.) Still other popular trips were the "moonlight" and the "autumn leaf" railroad excursions.

Special trains en route to Ward dropped off groups at the railroad-owned picnic ground and pavilion at Mont Alto. When demanding patrons insisted on a lake for rowing, the building was moved by the Colorado & Northwestern railroad to Glacier Lake, along its branch to Eldora.

Tourists loved their mountain railroad. Well-dressed passengers from this 1901 railroad excursion threw a snowball toward the camera. Photo by J. B. Sturtevant. Carnegie Branch Library for Local History, Boulder Historical Society Collection.

Ca. 1903, the first of the Ward area resorts, Stapp's Lake Lodge, opened to the public. According to legend, Isaac Stapp, founder of the resort, was struck with the beauty of the area while bear hunting in the 1880s. Another man in his party also showed an interest in the land. In the middle of the night, Stapp got on his horse and took off for the land office, then located in Central City. He filed a claim on 160 acres early the next morning, just as his rival arrived in the town.

When breathless tourists got off the train at the Ward depot, twenty-six miles and four thousand feet higher than Boulder, they piled into tallyhos. These sixteen-passenger stagecoaches were pulled by four horses. The main route north took them through Chipmunk Gulch and Quigleyville, part of the wagon road built in 1872 between Ward and Jamestown.

Soon the Lodge of the Pines, Glacier View Lodge, and the Peaceful Valley resort were in business as well. Travelers also stayed at the C & N, the Columbia, and the Utica Hotels in Ward. Railroad brochures from 1905 advertised daily stage connections and mail service from Ward to Stapp's Lake and on to Allen's Park (early spelling was two words).

Travelers out for a day on the Moffat Road also threw snowballs toward the camera. Pettem collection.

11

Also catering to tourists was the Denver, Northwestern & Pacific Railway, known as the "Moffat Road." Fighting snowbanks most of the year, standard gauge trains surmounted the Continental Divide at Rollins Pass, west of Rollinsville, from 1904 to 1927. Tourists boarded the trains in Denver for a ride to Corona, the station at the summit, in order to have their photograph taken "snowballing" in July.

More information on the Switzerland Trail and the Moffat Road will be found in corresponding sections in this book.

THE AGE OF THE AUTOMOBILE
(WARD TO ESTES PARK)

Once communities were established and people had a way to get there, tourism flourished. The western boundary of Boulder and Gilpin Counties was, and still is, the Continental Divide, that continuous crest of the Rocky Mountains which separates the water drainages of the East and the West. Everyone wanted a better view of the "Great Snowy Range," which extended from James Peak north to Longs Peak and Mt. Meeker.

Meanwhile, while gold and silver were being mined in Boulder and Gilpin Counties, and the tourists had discovered the railroads, the town of Estes Park had been settled as a resort community. Since it was out of the mineralized area, no mining activity occurred, and, consequently, no railroad ever reached the town. The Hotel Stanley was opened in 1909 by F. O. Stanley. He, along with his twin brother, F. E. Stanley, invented the Stanley Steamer Mountain Wagon in order to transport hotel guests to Estes Park from the railroad depots in Lyons and Loveland, and, as soon as the Peak to Peak Highway improved, from Ward.

The mountain wagons were larger and more rugged than the regular Stanley Steamer automobiles already in use in much of the country. Since the Stanley vehicles ran on steam instead of an internal combustion engine, they were almost silent. These mountain wagons seated eleven passengers and the driver on leather-covered seats of springs and horsehair which could be folded up to accommodate large trunks and other luggage. The vehicles had a 136-inch wheelbase, and were stunning with their shiny black bodies and bright red convertible tops.

F. O. Stanley is seated in the back on the right in this photo of one of his Stanley Steamer Mountain Wagons. The steam-powered vehicle is parked in front of the Stanley Hotel in Estes Park. Pettem collection.

Stanley Steamer automobiles and mountain wagons were particularly suited to the mountain terrain. In defense of his invention, F. O. Stanley wrote, "One of the chief advantages of the Stanley is its ease of operation. There is no risky rushing at hills and water bars, no dangerous taking of curves at high speed, and no noisy racing of the motor. The abundance of reserve power always at the command of the operator enables him to pick his way up the rough, stoney hills, and to slow down around blind curves."

Although they didn't have radiators, Stanley Steamers still needed water at regular intervals in order to make steam. In 1912, the mountain wagons were equipped with condensers, enabling the automobiles to go several hundred miles, instead of just fifty, before refilling with water. The same year, however, Cadillac became the first automobile with an internal combustion engine to install a self-starter. No longer would drivers have to crank-start their gasoline-powered cars, or spend ten to twenty minutes firing up the boilers of their steam-powered automobiles. But change didn't come overnight. Stanley Steamer mountain wagons continued to be used on the Ward to Estes Park auto road throughout the teens.

By 1912, steam-powered mountain wagons and automobiles of various makes were replacing some of the horse-drawn vehicles. It was time to work on the roads. The Boulder County Commissioners advertised for bids for the construction of an eight-mile section of a "scenic highway between Ward and Estes Park." This was part of the thirty-mile road past the Peaceful Valley resort and over what is now Boulder County 105 and 105J.

Promotional booklets in 1916 praised the improved route as the "Highline" as well as the "Skyline" Drive. Peaceful Valley's owner wrote, "No more inspiring views of mountain parks, pine-clad slopes, and snow-capped peaks are to be enjoyed than those from the Skyline Drive on the Nederland-Ward-Estes Park Highway. The road circles and climbs among the hills for miles, always above eight thousand feet elevation with a great array of snow-clad peaks ever forming an imposing background - Longs, James, Albion, Jasper, and Audubon included in the view."

Less in use at the time was a single-lane dirt road which extended from Peaceful Valley to the town of Raymond and on down South Saint Vrain Canyon. At Raymond, a road also went to Gresham and Jamestown while another went straight up Stanley Hill (named for homesteader G. B. Stanley), and connected with the Highline/Skyline Road to Allens Park and Estes Park.

Soon, many tourists owned their own automobiles. Traveling in the mountains was no longer limited to the train, stagecoach, or touring car. Families could venture out on their own.

People no longer had to depend on public transportation when they had automobiles of their own. Carnegie Branch Library for Local History, Boulder Historical Society Collection.

"Yoo-hoo point" above Peaceful Valley ca. 1922, and, below, in 1996. Carnegie Branch Library for Local History, Boulder Historical Society collection. Photo below by author.

Drivers of Model T Fords joined the traffic on the new road, but had a lot of trouble with overheating engines and boiling-over radiators. An old-timer who remembered those days said, "It was stop every little ways, go down to the creek for water, fill the radiator, and start up again." Often, Model Ts had to back up steep hills, as they had more power in reverse.

Eugene Parsons, in his 1911 *Guidebook to Colorado,* wrote, "Travel is an educator largely because history has left its footprints. The motorist will derive more enjoyment from his sightseeing if he occasionally takes a lay-off and turns some of the leaves of Colorado's fascinating annals. He should know something, at least, of the romance of mining. The traveler on the open road, who has a spark of imagination, can people the mountains with figures of explorers, trappers, hunters, and gold-seekers."

SCENERY (AND GOOD ROADS) MADE THEM STAY

Colorado learned early to cater to the tourist. The secret was in building better roads. Soon a "Good Roads Conference" was held in Denver. Recommendations were made to use convict labor from the state penitentiary. Conferees determined that "A system of good state roads would result in an immediate increase of tourist traffic in the state, with millions of dollars annually flowing into the hands of our people as a result of their expenditures while here."

They continued, "Every summer hordes of wealthy people from all parts of the United States would ship their cars [via railroad] to this state to indulge their penchant for motoring. There is little use in kicking about our wealthy classes going to Europe each year when they should spend their money at home."

Soon there would be another drawing card for the tourism industry. In the summer of 1912, R. B. Marshall, chief geographer of the United States Geological Survey, took a surveying party over the Continental Divide west of Estes Park to Grand Lake, then returned over Arapaho Pass through Eldora, north to Ward, and back to Estes Park. He proposed that 700 square miles be set aside for a Rocky Mountain National Park. The boundaries included those presently within the park as well as sections of Boulder and Grand Counties now in the Indian Peaks Wilderness.

Bear Lake, in the newly-created Rocky Mountain National Park, offered quiet and serenity. Pettem collection.

Marshall was enthusiastic and stated, "At first view, as one beholds the scene in awe and amazement, the effect is as of an enormous painting, a vast panorama stretching away for illimitable distances; gradually this idea of distance disappears, the magnificent work of nature seems to draw nearer and nearer, reduced apparently by an unseen microscope to the refinement of a delicate cameo."

Naturalist and Longs Peak Inn owner Enos Mills, who had envisioned a national park for some time, then lobbied the United States Congress to transfer part of the Colorado National Forest (now Roosevelt National Forest) to the National Park Service. In the end, the final park was not as large as Marshall or Mills had wanted.

The opening of Rocky Mountain National Park in 1915 coincided with an influx of tourists who had planned to vacation in Europe, but had to change their plans because of the World War. Although the war's effects were largely unfelt by the sightseers, tungsten mines and mills in the Nederland area were out-producing all others in the world to supply this needed hardening-agent for steel. The Switzerland Trail, then operated by the Denver, Boulder & Western railroad, continued to serve the area.

Many tourists still came on the train. Beginning in 1915, travelers could buy package tours which took them on the train from Denver to Ward, then they continued by Stanley Steamer from Ward to Estes Park. The next year, brochures advertised this "Rocky Mountain National Park Route" as the "grandest combination railroad and auto trip in all the West." After "scenic thrills" on the narrow gauge, and lunch in Ward, visitors completed their trip on the "new Ward-Estes Park Auto Route."

Trains left Denver at 8:00 am and reached Ward at 12:31pm. Passengers continuing on to Estes Park arrived there at 3:45 p.m. Round trip fare was $9.60, a sizable sum in those days. Travelers were encouraged to stop and stay along the way at resorts including Peaceful Valley, Allens Park, Copeland Lake, Hewes-Kirkwood Inn, The Columbines, and Longs Peak Inn. Brochures stated "Chauffeur a stop-over for the resort at which you desire to stop; spend such time there as you wish, and then continue your journey to your destination without additional cost. In doing this, you have not only taken the trip of your life, but you have avoided the expense of a side trip from Estes Park, as no doubt you had included a part of this very trip in your itinerary on side trips to be taken during your stay in the Park." Rates at the resorts averaged $14.00 to $20.00 per week, including meals.

Road improvements continued to be top priority. More and more families were traveling on their own. A 1917 newspaper stated, "The automobile traffic to Colorado is expected to be much greater this year than last. Roads are to be improved throughout the state and railroad crossings are to be more carefully safeguarded."

In 1919, a new road was constructed between Ward and Nederland. Most of it followed the general route of the earlier road except for the section through Puzzler, a mining camp on the Switzerland Trail. Instead of going down to Left Hand Canyon between Ward and Puzzler, the new road wound its way above and west of the railroad.

That same year, 1919, the narrow gauge railroad was abandoned. The tungsten boom was over, the railroad was losing money, and a flood washed out many bridges and miles of track. Tourists were so enthused with their new automobiles that they didn't seem to notice. Over forty thousand motor cars entered Rocky Mountain National Park, an all-time record. The next year people could drive their own automobiles up the newly-completed Fall River Road to the top of the Continental Divide. A recent hit song was "Come Away With Me Lucille, In My Merry Oldsmobile."

The Fall River Road was completed to the Continental Divide in 1920. Courtesy Daily Camera.

Parsons, in his *Guidebook,* cautioned, "Motoring in the mountains is different from motoring on the plains....A stage coach drawn by horses can ascend steep burro trails and hang on where an auto would lose its grip and topple over into a frowning abyss. The driver should avoid a high rate of speed, even when one of the party has been over the ground before...

Use an electric horn to avoid cramping of hands; keep sounding the horn at short intervals. It will prevent accidents."

Tourist brochures continued to push the Peak to Peak region. In 1921 visitors were told, "Boulder County has all kinds of scenery served up to suit the tastes of all comers. We are expecting you next summer to come and see."

GATEWAY TO THE GLACIERS

South of Rocky Mountain National Park and west of the towns of Nederland, Ward, and Peaceful Valley are the Indian Peaks, all over 12,000 feet. Named by the National Geographic Society, they include Ogallala, Paiute, Pawnee, Shoshoni, Apache, Navajo, and Arikaree. Between North and South Arapaho Peaks, on the eastern slope of the Continental Divide, is the Arapaho Glacier. In the 1920s it became a tourist attraction.

Automobile tourism, both in groups and by individual families, was in full swing. Who needed the mountain railroad when the Glacier Transportation Company brought hordes of travelers in modern seven-passenger cars, and personally escorted them on horseback to the Arapaho Glacier! "The big snow bank," as it was called, turned out to be a moving glacier. Credited with its discovery were Herbert N. Wheeler of the United States Forest Service and his brother-in-law, D. M. Andrews, a Boulder nurseryman, when they walked across it in search of dogtooth violet bulbs.

Wheeler wrote, "We began climbing up a hill of small rocks, and very soon [noticed] ice under and between the rocks, finally reaching the top of that declivity and onto the ice. As we proceeded, we came to cracks in the ice, at first two or three inches across and then several feet across. It filled the whole cirque on the east side of the two Arapaho Peaks, and was at least a half mile wide, and extended that far from the foot of the peaks. To be sure, it is the remnant of a sizable glacier that extended far down into the foothills, scouring out the canon and leaving lakes in its bed that are now the water supply for the city of Boulder."

People were curious about "the big snow bank" which turned out to be the Arapaho Glacier. Courtesy Daily Camera.

Fred Fair, Boulder's city engineer, came upon two more glaciers on the west side of the Continental Divide. He named these the Fair and Isabelle Glaciers after himself and his wife. They overlook a deep ice-carved valley called the Hellhole.

In 1922, Fair and others discovered the Peck Glacier, subsequently named for A. S. Peck of the United States Forest

Service. The Saint Vrain Glacier may have been located by United States Government engineers in the 1890s, but it wasn't made public until 1912. Other smaller glaciers on the east side include the Henderson Glacier, the Navaho Peak Glacier, and the Arikaree Ice Field.

To encourage tourism, Boulder became known as the "Gateway to the Glaciers." Druggist, Eben G. Fine, who represented the Boulder Chamber of Commerce, traveled around the country and publicized the glaciers with over 3,000 lectures and lantern slide shows. In an effort to lure even more tourists, Enos Mills wrote a series of articles on the Arapaho Glacier for midwestern newspapers.

What really brought in the crowds was an advertising campaign by officials of the Burlington Railroad, headquartered in Chicago. The railroad adopted the glacier trip as one of their main attractions of 1921. Ticket agents were sent from the "windy city" to see first hand the "solid river of ice." A railroad official stated, "In thirty-six hours from Chicago, people can see more than the Alps provide in thrills and mountain grandeur."

Intending to capitalize on this publicity, Fred Fair obtained permission from the Boulder County Commissioners to build a road to the overlook, called the "saddle," above Arapaho Glacier. The scenic lookout would be complete with shelter house and refreshment stand. The first leg of the road, to the present Rainbow Lakes campground, was completed in 1924. Realizing that this project would cost at least $100,000, Fair teamed up with a Colorado Springs millionaire who proposed a toll road. By 1925, the Arapaho Glacier was nationally known and had been featured in one hundred fifty magazines around the country.

Soon everyone had to climb on, or under, the Arapaho Glacier. Above, Carnegie Branch Library for Local History, Boulder Historical Society Collection; below, courtesy Daily Camera.

Fair operated the Glacier Route automobile line which got people "into the glacier region" at Rainbow Lakes, but not yet overlooking Arapaho Glacier as he had hoped. To experience the glacier first-hand, tourists were taken on horseback from "Arapaho Camp." Sightseers from Denver boarded the electrically-powered Denver & Interurban Railroad. When they arrived in Boulder, they piled into waiting automobiles for the ride up Boulder Canyon. Soon the tourists arrived at their camp where they were served coffee and sandwiches. They reached the glacier on horseback by noon, stayed an hour, then rode back to the camp where they were fed dinner. Again they boarded the automobiles for their return to Boulder and Denver.

As part of the glacier promotion, the Denver & Interurban Railroad offered a thousand dollar prize to the first aviator who would land an airplane on the slopes of Saint Vrain Glacier. A lanky young barnstormer and stunt flyer known as "Slim" begged for the job, but Fred Fair took one look at his small rickety plane, and turned him down. No one else volunteered.

"Slim" turned out to be Charles Lindbergh. After he completed his first transatlantic flight, and landed in Paris, the *Denver Post* proposed naming a Colorado peak in his honor. Fair suggested a 12,000-foot pinnacle, near the Saint Vrain Glacier. Although he originally named it Lindbergh Peak, it soon became Lone Eagle Peak, as the U. S. Board of Geographic Names ruled against naming a peak for a living individual.

The glacier publicity alarmed promoters of the recently-created Rocky Mountain National Park. The Colorado Mountain Club and the Rocky Mountain Climbers Club tried to expand the Park southward to include Arapaho Glacier as originally proposed by geographer Marshall. This, the club members felt, would "keep the area free from spoliation by the greed of commercial interests or irresponsible transient tourists." President Coolidge's Coordinating Commission also favored expanding Rocky Mountain National Park.

By the time of the road controversy, people in Boulder were drinking water which drained directly from the Arapaho Glacier into a group of lakes and then into Silver Lake, a city-owned and protected watershed. Some Boulderites raised questions on the effect of the proposed road on the watershed's sanitation. Others were more interested in encouraging tourism. Frank Eckel, Secretary of the Boulder Chamber of Commerce, said, "Let the [road] builders go through, and bid them godspeed." A Boulder *Daily Camera* editorial stated, "If the glacier is one of God's masterpieces, are we justified in denying sight of it to any of His children?"

Most Boulder residents agreed that they didn't want "their" glacier in Rocky Mountain National Park. The editor of the Boulder *News-Herald* was adamant that Boulder itself should purchase the glacier. In 1927, he wrote, "If the City of Boulder gets possession of the acres in question, it is certain that the czaristic National Park Service will never get them. If it does not take advantage of its opportunity to buy this acreage, it has no real protection against the future whims and policies of federal bureaucracy. The *News-Herald* believes strongly in the doctrine of state and local rights when applied to such vital issues as state control over its own roads and a city's control over its watershed."

Torn between the economic benefits of promoting tourism and protecting Boulder's water supply, Boulder city officials advised the purchase of the 3,869-acre area from the federal government for $1.25 per acre. This was accomplished in 1929.

Fred Fair, however, was still promoting his Glacier Route auto line. On July 4, 1929, he brought a truckload of snow from the mountains to Boulder. "Pretty girls" threw snowballs from the truck during that year's Independence Day parade. Accompanying them was a float of a mountain scene featuring, not surprisingly, a glacier.

The Council decided to fence off the watershed and close it to public use. The hopes of a glacier toll road were doomed. With the glacier the sole source of Boulder's drinking water, fountains all over the city were inscribed with the words, "Pure Cold Water from the Boulder-Owned Arapaho Glacier." The only surviving fountain with this inscription today is in the lobby of the Hotel Boulderado at 13th and Spruce Streets in Boulder. Now the inscription is misleading, as only part of Boulder's water supply still comes from the Arapaho Glacier.

Beginning in 1939, the Boulder Chamber of Commerce led annual summer hikes to the saddle (overlook site) so people could still have an opportunity to view the Arapaho Glacier. The group carpooled in a caravan up Boulder Canyon. They rode through Eldora to the base camp at Fourth of July campground where they were served breakfast. Participants were told that while the climb wasn't treacherous, the three to four-hour uphill hike was a "long, hard, exhausting pull."

Two hundred people participated that first year including the mayor, the city manager, the superintendent of schools, the president and secretary of the Chamber of Commerce, several members of the University faculty, the Boulder County Commissioners, a state senator, newspaper reporters, and many prominent business and professional men and women.

Upon reaching the saddle, just below the final leg of the climb up South Arapaho Peak, the Rocky Mountain Rescue Group presented a rock climbing exhibition. Some of the hikers descended onto the glacier to slide and throw snowballs. After they returned, the group headed down the way they had come and enjoyed a hot dinner at their base camp.

For many years the Boulder Chamber of Commerce led hikes to the saddle overlooking Arapaho Glacier, which is out of view to the right. Mount Neva is in the background in this 1962 photo. Courtesy Daily Camera.

Today, walking on Arapaho Glacier is off-limits, and the group hikes have been discontinued, but individual hikers can still get a close-up look at the glacier by climbing to the saddle (overlook) from either the Fourth of July or Rainbow Lakes campgrounds.

TOURISM CONTINUES

Many would-be tourists were kept at home in the 1930s by the Great Depression. If they could afford to travel, they found that the Peak to Peak Highway was still unpaved. In 1926, the section of road between Ward, Peaceful Valley, and Raymond had been the first to be widened from one to two lanes. Just north of Ward the road was rerouted higher on the mountainside, and bypassed the early road through Chipmunk Gulch. The Highline/Skyline Drive, praised so highly a decade before, was abandoned in favor of the improved road along the Middle Saint Vrain Creek through Raymond.

A newspaper reporter wrote, "The road constructed between Raymond thru Peaceful Valley to Ward, and the contemplated double-tracked highway between Ward and Nederland, will add another splendid circle trip for Boulder tourists. The trip can be made easily and comfortably in one day and will be unparalleled in the state of Colorado. The vista over the highway from Peaceful Valley to Ward and from Ward to Nederland is not equaled in the state, if not in the West. The motorist will drive in safety over a splendid mountain road to within 1,500 feet in altitude from the crest of the Continental Divide." The grade was also reduced between Raymond and Allenspark (one word today).

In 1930, the whole route between Nederland and Raymond was declared a state highway, as it connected existing state roads to the north and south. The Boulder County Commissioners wanted the "scenic drive [to] be one continuous system." Rocky Mountain National Park's Trail Ridge Road opened in 1932 and continued over the Continental Divide. For tourists fortunate enough to leave home, it was a good time to travel.

In 1935, the Nederland to Ward section finally became two-laned. Some of the sharp curves were removed, but the highway's route stayed essentially the same. By the time the Depression was over, World War II was underway. Gasoline and tires were rationed, again keeping many people at home.

In the late 1940s and early 1950s, tourist travel hit all-time highs. Sections of the Peak to Peak Highway received an "oil-paving." Gasoline was cheap and plentiful. Americans were urged to "See the USA in [their] Chevrolet," or whatever family car they owned.

Minor route changes were made in 1958 to remove additional sharp turns and steep grades. New sections of highway bypassed the towns of Allenspark, Meeker Park, and Ferncliff. A cut between Ward and Peaceful Valley saved three-quarters of a mile but eliminated what Colorado Mountain Club members felt was the best view of the mountains. They pointed out that the Peak to Peak Highway was used as a scenic drive by thousands of tourists who photograph the grandeur of the mountains. "This tourist visitation is of vital importance to our economy," club members stated, but their argument fell on deaf ears. Further corners were cut to speed the motorist on his way.

In 1969, Colorado Governor John Love's road committee recommended renaming the Boulder County portion of the Peak to Peak Highway as the "Eisenhower Highway" as a memorial to the late President. The suggestion was turned down so that the tunnel then being drilled under the Continental Divide, on Interstate 70, would receive the President's name. In 1989, the Peak to Peak Highway was designated a scenic byway.

In his guidebook, Parsons eloquently praised automobile travel in the Rockies. He wrote, "Speeding over a picturesque touring-road on the roof of the world stirs the spirit's inner deeps. The magnitude of a mountain chain affects the imagination. The Rockies hold a spell for all who come and sojourn for a while in their midst. A mountain drive is an unforgettable experience. The man who has motored through scenic Colorado once, will want to come again and tour one route after another."

Tourists stop along an unidentified section of the road. Pettem collection.

Black Hawk was a busy milling town and railroad center in its early days. Pettem collection.

PART II

BLACK HAWK AND CENTRAL CITY

When gold mining ran the economy of the Central City district, dozens of gold mills were set up in Black Hawk, on North Clear Creek. Even gold ore from Ward and Gold Hill, in the early 1860s, was hauled through what is now Nederland and Rollinsville to be processed in the "mill city of the Rockies." However, far more gold came from the mines in Gregory and Russell Gulches, Nevadaville, and other surrounding areas.

Besides the town's many mills, the first commercially-successful gold smelter in what became Colorado was built in Black Hawk in 1867 by Nathaniel P. Hill. Later he became a United States senator. Most of the area's bankers, lawyers, and storekeepers located in the nearby town of Central City.

In 1872, Colorado Territory's first narrow gauge railroad, the Colorado Central, chugged into Black Hawk. The following year, President Ulysses S. Grant and his family arrived on the train, then took a carriage to Central City. When Grant alighted in front of the Teller House Hotel, he was ushered onto a walkway of silver bricks made from recent strikes at Caribou. It was said that gold was too ordinary for such a dignitary.

Another branch of the Colorado Central Railroad was extended up Clear Creek Canyon to Georgetown in 1877. A year later, the Black Hawk route twisted and turned along four and one-half miles of grade in order to reach Central City, only one steep mile uphill.

A 175-foot railroad bridge crossed Black Hawk's main street and passed the upstairs rooms of Baby Doe and her first husband Harvey Doe. Later Baby Doe divorced Harvey to marry Horace Tabor whose fortune in silver mining was made in Leadville. The story of Tabor's wealth and subsequent downfall has been memorialized in the opera "The Ballad of Baby Doe."

In Central City, the solid stone Teller Opera House, named for Senator Henry M. Teller, opened in 1878. When Central City's population dropped in the 1920s, the opera house fell into disuse, then was reopened in 1932. Lillian Gish, Faye Emerson, Helen Hayes, and Shirley Booth all have performed there. Next door, in the still-standing Teller House Bar, the "Face on the Barroom Floor" represents the ballad of the same name. It was painted on the floor by Herndon Davis who also painted the murals in the Colorado State Capitol Building.

The opera house and many of the other brick and stone buildings in Central City replaced the original and hastily-built wooden structures of the early 1860s. A fire which swept through the town in 1874 was followed by a ban on new wooden buildings.

Central City and Black Hawk are part of a National Historic District. Exteriors of the existing historic buildings are to remain unchanged. Most of the mill buildings have long since disappeared and have recently been replaced with casinos. Most of the interiors of the other buildings have been extensively remodeled. Since small-stakes gambling was legalized in 1991, the towns' economies have revolved around blackjack and poker games and the ever-present slot machines. Part of the profits make up the grant money provided by the Colorado Historical Society for the preservation of historic buildings all over the state.

The one building in Black Hawk which, so far, has not changed is the Lace House at 161 Main Street. It was built ca. 1863 by Lucien K. Smith who operated the toll gate (and saloon) at Black Hawk for travelers taking the Enterprise Road to Denver. The ornate wooden home, with its "gingerbread," pointed-arched windows, and steeply-pitched roof is an excellent example of "carpenter Gothic" architecture.

The Lace House is now owned by the city of Black Hawk and is open as a museum. Photo by author, 1996.

Rollins's barn is above at left. Carnegie Branch Library for Local History, Boulder. Below, the barn is now the Stage Stop Inn, 1996 photo by Clara Pettem.

ROLLINSVILLE AND THE MOFFAT ROAD

The small town of Rollinsville was named for its founder, John Quincy Adams Rollins. After amassing quite an estate of mining property and farm lands in the area, he entered into a race with surveyor and engineer Captain Edward L. Berthoud to see who would be the first to complete a wagon road from the east side of the Continental Divide into Middle Park. Both men envisioned Middle Park as a destination for tourists and realized the potential for increased commerce and trade.

The Rollinsville and Middle Park Wagon Road was completed first, in 1873. But Rollins's initial success was short-lived. Merchants at Idaho Springs, Empire, and Georgetown continued to improve the Berthoud Pass route (now U.S. 40) so that their towns, not Rollinsville, would become the supply center for Middle Park. Rollins's efforts were not entirely in vain as parts of his wagon road became the right-of-way for the railroad soon to be known as the "Moffat Road."

The man behind this railroad was David Halliday Moffat, Jr. He served as president of the First National Bank of Denver, then the leading bank in the Rocky Mountains. Through the bank and his numerous investments in mines, railroads, and other ventures, he played a leading role in Colorado's development from 1860 to 1911.

In 1902, Moffat was sixty-three years old. He might have retired and enjoyed the fruits of his labor, but instead launched his most ambitious business venture, the Denver, Northwestern & Pacific Railway. Moffat's goal was to cross the Front Range of the Rockies northwest of Denver, tap the coal and agricultural areas of Middle Park and North Park, and build on to Salt Lake City and San Francisco. It was an extraordinarily ambitious, if not speculative, project.

The "Moffat Road" followed the route of the wagon road laid out by John Quincy Adams Rollins. Pettem collection.

The railroad was capitalized at $20 million. Denver's business elite invested heavily although the company's board consisted principally of the officers of the First National Bank. Construction began immediately, but the difficult terrain on the "hill route" west of Rollinsville slowed construction and drove up costs. The key was surmounting the Continental Divide at Rollins Pass. Moffat's engineers recognized the need for a six-mile tunnel under the divide, but found it financially impossible at the time. They laid the rail instead over the 11,600-foot pass. Costs mounted dramatically as heavy winter snows disrupted service. In fact, almost half of the railroad's operational budget was used to fight snow.

The tracks over the summit of Rollins Pass made the Moffat Road the highest standard gauge line in the world. In the summer, for years to come, tourists rode the train to "the top of the world." The station at the top was named Corona, which is Spanish for "crown." In 1913, a hotel and restaurant were built just to the north of the station.

A trip on the Denver, Northwestern & Pacific was a ride to the "top of the world." Pettem collection.

The railroad needed more than tourists to survive. Unfortunately, the Union Pacific Railroad's line between Cheyenne and Salt Lake City took most of the east-west trade. Moffat made numerous trips to New York to try to obtain more capital, but died suddenly and heavily in debt in 1911. At the time, the railroad had only reached as far west as Steamboat Springs. The Moffat Road was forced into receivership, but eventually emerged as the Denver & Salt Lake Railway. Finally it merged into the Denver & Rio Grande.

In the 1920s, private and public funds built the Moffat Tunnel under the Continental Divide which eliminated the costly passage over the mountains. When the Moffat Tunnel opened in 1927, it cut the average running time for passenger trains from two and one-half hours (in good weather) to twelve minutes. In 1935, the Denver & Rio Grande Western began routing the famous Panoramic and Exposition Flyer trains through the tunnel and west via the Dotsero Cutoff. Ultimately they were succeeded by the Pioneer Zephyr, California Zephyr and the Prospector.

The railroad tracks over the pass were torn up in the 1930s. Then, in the 1950s, the United States Forest Service, along with Gilpin, Grand, and Boulder Counties decided to maintain the road for auto travel between Rollinsville, on the east side, and Winter Park, on the west. In 1979, however, a rockfall in the Needle's Eye Tunnel near the top of the pass forced the road to close.

Since 1983, the nonprofit Rollins Pass Restoration Association has raised money to repair the tunnel and reopen the road. Boulder County, whose jurisdiction covers the Needle's Eye, donated more than $60,000, while the association raised matching funds from individuals as well as Gilpin and Grand

Counties. Four hundred seventy rock bolts, eight and ten feet in length, were set by epoxy into drilled holes holding 5,000 square feet of welded wire mesh in the rock walls.

The Needle's Eye tunnel reopened in 1988, but was closed again by another rockfall in 1990. Currently, on the east side, the road is blocked above Forest Lakes, within walking distance of the Needles Eye Tunnel and the summit.

> *To follow the "Hill Route" to the Forest Lakes turn-off, turn west (left if you're driving north) off the Peak to Peak Highway (Colorado 119) at Rollinsville and follow County Road 149. You'll pass through the site of Tolland, once a popular resort. At 7.5 miles from Rollinsville, take the sharp uphill turn to the right just before the East Portal of the Moffat Tunnel. Then begin the "Giant's Ladder," a series of switchbacks which allowed the railroad to remain at a four per cent or lower grade. Eventually you'll reach the circular Yankee Doodle Lake before the roadblock above Forest Lakes. It's a short walk from there to the Needle's Eye Tunnel where you can continue to the site of Corona, on the summit of the pass.*
>
> *The road is rough, but passable by highway vehicles.*

False-fronted commercial buildings such as this one with decorative shingles are within Eldora's Historic District. Photo by author, 1996.

ELDORA, SULPHIDE FLATS, AND THE LAKE ELDORA AREA

Beginning in 1897, zealous promoters pushed Eldora as "another Cripple Creek." Neither before nor since has the town had so much mining activity. Despite the dreams of its founders, Eldora never produced much gold.

John H. Kemp located the Happy Valley placer claim in 1891. There were occasional gold discoveries over the next few years, then, in 1897, came a sudden two-year flurry of activity. Newcomers packed the stagecoaches that rumbled into town each day. The population jumped from a few miners to over one thousand. At first, accommodations were scarce and the only places to sleep were the floors of Eldora's eleven saloons. Bartenders spread thick layers of sawdust for their boarders. Often breakfast was a shot of whiskey.

The town was originally called Happy Valley after Kemp's claim. Then it became Camp Eldorado, complete with a post office, but missing mail kept turning up in Eldorado, California. Those in the Colorado town agreed to shorten the name to Eldora.

Eldora's original plat reflected the social mores of the day. When the town was laid out, dance halls and bawdy houses ("with fourteen beautiful girls to serve you," claimed promotional literature) were required to locate across the creek from the business and residential areas. A real estate frenzy was responsible for most of the town's early buildings. Eldora's quick growth supported several hotels. The largest was the Gold Miner Hotel, built in the winter of 1897 and 1898.

Community activities were enhanced with the twenty-piece men's silver cornet band. Fourth of July celebrations centered on rock-drilling contests between miners who came from Central City, Ward, Gold Hill, and other camps to compete with the men of Eldora. Festivities continued with supper at midnight, and dancing which typically lasted until the morning.

Teamsters hauled in supplies to the bustling gold camp of Eldora. Carnegie Branch Library for Local History, Boulder Historical Society Collection.

For awhile, Eldora's outlook was bright. Early gold production came from mines such as the Enterprise, Village Belle, Virginia, Terror, Bonanza, Clara, Gold Coin, and Bird's

Nest, with big hopes for the Mogul Tunnel driven deep into Spencer Mountain.

Mills were built to process the ores from the mines. The biggest mill was a chlorination mill built by Neil Bailey to handle the ore from the Enterprise mine. Unfortunately, Bailey discovered that his process was unsuited for Eldora's ores, the mill lost a lot of gold, and Bailey's financial backer in New York perished with his entire family in a house fire. In desperation, Bailey turned to his relatives who were prosperous farmers in upstate New York. Smitten with gold fever, they sold off their farms, moved to Eldora, and allowed Bailey to pour their money into the mill. But, even then, no amount of experimentation increased the yield of gold.

Then Bailey's situation got worse. Disgruntled employees demanded overdue paychecks. When Bailey couldn't or wouldn't pay, his workers allegedly set his house on fire, then someone shot him in the arm as he tried to put out the blaze. The Marshal arrived, rescued Bailey, and managed to get the fire under control, but a few days later Bailey's gunshot wound became infected and he died.

Although Bailey's assailants had now become murderers, many residents of Eldora, according to newspaper reports, thought that Bailey "got what was coming to him." When brought to trial, each one claimed to be somewhere else at the time of the crime. The jury agreed, and all were acquitted.

The boom had passed when Colorado & Northwestern president Samuel B. Dick finally succeeded in extending the railroad line to Eldora in January, 1905. However, Dick firmly believed that the railroad, which he envisioned crossing the Continental Divide into Middle Park, would revitalize the slow production from the Mogul Tunnel. Unfortunately for him,

Eldora's gold-bearing veins were too small, and one by one the mines closed down. Some gold mining continued off and on until the United States entered the World War in 1917.

What the town lacked in gold production it made up with scenery. The railroad lost no time in offering its "wild flower excursions" on which tourists to Eldora were treated to the "grandest panoramic view in the world." In 1918, members of the Rocky Mountain Climbers Club left Boulder on the train and got off in Eldora in time for lunch. They then hiked seven miles to the Fourth of July mine where they set up camp. The next day they hiked to the Arapaho Glacier overlook, where some of the party continued on to climb South Arapaho and then North Arapaho peaks. A second night was spent at the camp site before returning to Eldora and the train ride back to Boulder.

The crew of the Mogul Tunnel, ca. 1900. Bolton collection.

As automobile travel increased, Eldora was promoted as "the place to spend your vacation." In the 1920s, when tourism had solidly replaced mining as the town's economic base, new residents built additional summer cabins which they visited year after year. The usual slump came during the Depression, but Eldora was rediscovered in 1939 when the Boulder Chamber of Commerce led its carpool caravan through the town for the first of many annual hikes to Arapaho Glacier.

The Gold Miner Hotel looks much the same as in its early days. Today it's been reopened as a bed and breakfast. Photo by author, 1996.

In 1989, sixty-seven buildings in the town, including the Gold Miner Hotel, were formed into the Eldora Historic District and placed on the National Register of Historic Places. Eldora is significant, not only for its rustic turn-of-the-century architecture, but also because its community development is associated with the growth and decline of the region's metal mining industry and the beginnings of tourism in the late nineteenth and early twentieth centuries. Today the town is a quiet residential community.

SULPHIDE FLATS

During the boom days at Eldora, promoters tried hard to push the townsite of Sulphide Flats as "the inevitable business center of Eldora." Its location was the flat area to the north of County Road 130 just before entering Eldora. A stock prospectus said that "money invested in Sulphide will make you rich." Other literature pushed the paper town as follows--

"[Sulphide Flats would be] an ideal summer resort, with lakes filled with game fish, mountain drives, rippling brooklets, scenery that's an inspiration, air that's life, a spot perfumed with the mingled odors of countless wild flowers and the fragrance of evergreen pines, while all around the whistling of engines, the rumbling of ore wagons, and the rattling of stages filled with gay though determined fortune hunters who tell the story of the great gold mines of the Eldora district."

That was about as far as it got. Sulphide Flats never achieved its intended glory or prosperity. Perhaps its greatest claim to fame is that the railroad ran a temporary spur line from Sulphide Flats down the valley to the construction site of Barker Dam.

LAKE ELDORA AREA

The Lake Eldora area's origins grew out of the expected gold discoveries in Eldora. In 1898, former Colorado Governor

Alva Adams and a group of prominent businessmen bought Peterson Lake and the adjoining property on Spencer Mountain south of Eldora. They formed the Eldora Resort and Power Company, intending to supply Eldora with water and electrical power as well as operate a summer resort. Plans called for the construction of a railroad spur or an aerial tram up the mountain, neither of which materialized.

Peterson's Lake was renamed Lake Ha Ha Tonka meaning "limpid laughing water." Forty acres around the lake were platted into lots for summer homes. A newspaper account speculated that "overworked men and women, weary with the exactions of physical or mental toil, and worn with the friction of business or household cares, can come during the heated season and spend a period in the luxury of rest and recuperation...in an atmosphere cool and bracing, and yet of unclouded sunlight, amid scenes that forever charm the eye and gladden the soul." The crowds never came. All that resulted was the opening of Pine Log Lodge, billed for several years as a "charming family and fishing resort."

According to records left by author Jack Langley, Denver socialite Annie D. Morris bought the property in 1914. She built a vacation home called Dixie Lodge, and hired Japanese laborers to dam nearby Lake Eldora which she named Lake Kaanawha. Japanese-style bridges connected the islands formed by the rising water. Mrs. Morris used Dixie Lodge to entertain family and friends. After her death, the home was abandoned, and it burned in 1969.

Pine Log Lodge burned in the mid-1960s. All that remains of the "resort" today is the dam around Lake Eldora, the stone chimney of Dixie Lodge and a few scattered cabins.

In 1961, another group of businessmen organized Lake Eldora Corporation to build and operate a ski area. Throughout the years since, the skiable terrain has been expanded, and new lifts, lighting, and an extensive snow-making system have been installed. The area now is open from mid-November to early April, weather permitting. The area has a 1,400 foot vertical rise to an elevation of 10,600 feet. Its many trails include one that is two miles long. Lake Eldora also offers back country trails for cross-country skiing.

> To reach the Eldora area, turn west (left if you're driving north) off the Peak to Peak Highway (Colorado 119 and Colorado 72) onto County Road 130, just south of Nederland. In one and one-half miles, County Road 140 turns off to the left to Lake Eldora. Road 130 continues on to Eldora, with the site of Sulphide Flats on the right before entering the town.
>
> Hiking trails to Lost Lake, Woodland Lake, Jasper Lake, Devils Thumb Pass, and Diamond Lake start at the Hessie townsite, west of Eldora. A right turn at Hessie follows the North Fork of the Middle Boulder Creek to the Fourth of July (Buckingham) campground. Trails there lead to Diamond Lake, Arapaho Pass, Caribou Pass, and the Arapaho Glacier overlook.

NEDERLAND
(FORMERLY BROWNSVILLE, DAYTON, AND MIDDLE BOULDER)

Remembering the tungsten boom, an oldtimer said, "Nederland was just a madhouse. They slept up here in shifts, eight hours. One fellow would get up, another fellow got in before the bed got cold. Old John McRae put cots in the skating rink and operated round the clock. Everybody who had a spare room was renting it. People pitched tents and built shacks -- anything to live in."

Nederland is the only community in Boulder County to have experienced the boom and bust of three types of mining -- silver, gold, and tungsten. It also was a milling and freighting center located at the junction of the Peak to Peak Highway and Boulder Canyon. In Nederland, both Colorado 72 and Colorado 119 comprise the Peak to Peak Highway, with Colorado 119 following Boulder Canyon to Boulder.

One of the area's original gold seekers was Nathan W. Brown. The few claims he staked never amounted to much. With his wife Caroline, and their four children, he filed a forty-acre agricultural homestead along the Middle Boulder Creek. There the Browns built a two-story log cabin and opened their doors as innkeepers.

Their location, originally known as Brownsville, and then Dayton and Middle Boulder, soon became a stop on the wagon road between Black Hawk and Ward. After silver was discovered in Caribou, the freighters heading up from Boulder and the ore wagons going down stopped there too. The Browns found themselves in the middle of an important intersection.

THE SILVER BOOM

Brownsville (Dayton, Middle Boulder) began to thrive as a supply center when prospectors discovered a fabulous silver deposit at Caribou in 1869. Heavily-laden wagons rolled in with goods and machinery bound for the instant town. To process the silver ore, A. D. Breed built a ten-stamp mill at Caribou, but soon decided that Brownsville was a better location. The second Caribou Mill was built in the town in 1871. The mill consumed 250 cords of wood per month and employed eighteen men.

The Caribou Mill was rebuilt in Brownsville (Nederland). The building behind and to the right of the mill is the Hetzer House Hotel. Carnegie Branch Library for Local History, Boulder Historical Society Collection.

Before 1871, no road had extended all the way up Boulder Canyon. In 1866, road builders had succeeded in getting from Boulder to the foot of Magnolia Hill, then up through the town of Magnolia and on to Black Hawk. Three years later, Wells-Fargo & Co. stated their intention of running a stage line between Boulder and Black Hawk if a shorter route between the two towns could be built. During the winter, when Middle Boulder Creek was frozen in the "narrows" of Boulder Canyon, surveyors determined that a route up the canyon would be six miles shorter than the road through Magnolia. As a result, local businessmen quickly organized a stock company to build the toll road from the Magnolia turn-off to Brownsville.

The Boulder Canyon Road, with its thirty-three bridges, was completed to what was then called Middle Boulder (now Nederland) in 1871. Wells Fargo never put on the promised stages, but that made little difference. Lee and Walter Smith ran Concord stages daily, and a stage station known as the American House was built at the head of the narrows so that passengers could buy a meal when the drivers changed horses.

With the silver boom at Caribou in full swing, Middle Boulder quickly grew into an important stage stop and freighting center. Mail arrived daily from Central City and three times a week from Boulder. In addition to his official duties, the postman operated a grocery and dry goods store. Following the activity, merchants relocated from Black Hawk with a full stock of hardware and mining supplies. Physicians, lawyers, and other merchants flocked to the bustling community. Soon it had a sawmill, livery stable, and a school that doubled as a church. The residential section grew to over one hundred frame houses. The Hetzer House (Hotel), which burned in 1939, was "second to none in the hill country."

In 1873, Middle Boulder underwent its last name change. That year mining investors from Holland bought the Caribou Mill. They changed the name of the town to Nederland, meaning "lowland." It was low compared to Caribou, nestled high against the Continental Divide. The Dutch company went broke in 1878, but the name stuck and remains today.

Silver poured out of Caribou's mines until the mid-1880s, then the mining camp faded away and with it the bustle in the town of Nederland. In 1889, a visitor reported that the population consisted of only seven families, plus some stray stock and burros. The silver crash in 1893 finished off the last of the local silver mines and brought the milling and supply town of Nederland to a temporary standstill.

GOLD AND TUNGSTEN

Things weren't quiet for long. In 1897, the nearby town of Eldora went into its gold boom which revitalized Nederland. The Antlers Hotel (torn down in 1961) was built to attract the growing number of tourists but instead was overrun with gold-seeking prospectors. On the heels of the new gold rush came the tungsten boom.

For years, prospectors had been annoyed with an unfamiliar substance they called "that damned black iron." Not until 1900 did Sam Conger, who had made the initial discovery of silver at Caribou, identify it as tungsten ore -- tungsten being a rare metal used as a hardening agent in steel. Within the next few years, C. F. Lake built the Primos Mill two miles north of Nederland. Its foundations are still visible immediately on the west side of the Peak to Peak Highway across from its intersection with County Road 124E.

By 1910, Boulder County tungsten was known worldwide, and Nederland was the major United States producer. The outbreak of the World War a few years later created a tremendous demand for high speed tool steel and airplane engine valves. Prices surged tenfold, and the tungsten industry boomed as never before. The Caribou silver mill was renamed the Wolf Tongue, and revamped to produce the metal.

Other changes were coming to Nederland, too. Plans were made to construct Barker Dam and Reservoir just east of town. Its purpose was to collect water from Middle Boulder Creek, direct it into a twelve-mile gravity line between Nederland and Kossler Reservoir above Boulder, and let it run down a 9,647-foot penstock to the newly-built hydroelectric power plant in Boulder Canyon.

Construction got underway in 1907. To bring equipment and supplies to the dam site, the Colorado & Northwestern Railroad built a spur line from Sulphide Flats, just below Eldora. Before long, 600 to 700 men were at work along with 160 horses and mules, six locomotives, 150 dump cars, three 170-ton steam shovels, ten steam concrete mixers, and innumerable diamond drills, hoists, boilers, pumps, and aerial trams, along with more than 132,000 cubic yards of cement. When completed in 1910, Barker Dam stood 175 feet high by 720 feet long.

Before the lake was allowed to fill up, the railroad removed its spur line. Yet, at very low water, the railroad grade through the middle of what was once a meadow can still be seen.

Both tungsten mining and the construction of Barker Dam were good for Nederland's saloons and local businesses. Four- and six-horse teams hauled supplies from wholesalers in

Boulder and Black Hawk to retailers in Nederland. At the time, supplies also came by railroad as far as Cardinal (between Caribou and Nederland), then were hauled into Nederland on freight wagons.

In October, 1918, the influenza epidemic hit the county. Even the big Primos Mill had to shut down because there weren't enough well men to make up a shift. Then on November 11, 1918, came the armistice ending the World War. With it went the wartime demand for tungsten, although some tungsten ore was still mined in the 1920s and during the Depression. Mining continued, off and on, through the Korean Conflict in the early 1950s.

Despite all of its mining activities, Nederland was promoted as a tourist resort, especially in the 1920s. "Why not come up and live in a cottage at Nederland this summer?" urged one promotional booklet. "The surroundings are inspiring -- just the place for headquarters while you hike over the hills and through the valleys -- up among the perpetually snow-capped peaks of the Continental Divide." Read another, "The lakes are heavily stocked with many varieties of trout, and afford unequaled sport. Other lakes, scattered over the wild and broken country clear to the Divide, offer added inducements to the seeker for good angling. Even if you don't fish, it's great to spend the summer where the fishing's good!"

The Visitor Center in Nederland provides current tourist information on the area.

CARIBOU

The cold and snow are so relentless in Caribou that a newcomer once asked, "Just how long does the winter last here?" Back came the answer, "Don't know, I've only been here three years."

The mining boom at Caribou came a decade after the Pikes Peak gold rush. In the summer of 1869, as the story goes, a lone prospector hunted for elk rather than gold. He found neither, but stumbled across a rock outcropping that he couldn't identify. When it proved rich in silver, the word got out and the boom was on -- it was Colorado's first major silver rush.

The town of Caribou was laid out in 1870, but couldn't grow fast enough. Prospectors poured in from all quarters. Experienced miners, called "Cousin Jacks" crossed the Atlantic from Cornwall. Miners and merchants pitched tents before builders could put up boarding houses, stores, and saloons. Soon the town had hotels, billiard and dance halls, blacksmith shops, a stable, photographic gallery, church, numerous other businesses, and *The Caribou Post*, a weekly newspaper that served the quickly-growing town.

Soon there were tales of fabulous wealth. The miners who staked the Idaho claim reportedly took out more than six thousand dollars from a twenty-foot shaft in one month. The Caribou mine produced an estimated $8 million worth of silver and became one of Colorado's greatest silver producers. Other mines included the Trojan, Boulder County, Sovereign People, No-Name, Spencer, and Seven-Thirty. The mining world's attention also focused on Caribou when a magnificent collection of silver ore was displayed at the nation's Centennial Exposition in Philadelphia in 1876.

The Sherman House Hotel (center) dominated the town of Caribou in 1886. Pettem collection.

Even so, Caribou was a hard place in which to live. Besides the heavy snows at the nearly 10,000 elevation, the town was known as "the place where the winds are born." Disease also took its toll. Epidemics of scarlet fever and diphtheria took the lives of many of the children. Headstones of the era (now stolen or destroyed) were carved with epitaphs such as "This little bud to us was given, to bud on Earth and bloom in Heaven," and simply "Gone, but not forgotten."

But neither snow, wind, nor disease was as destructive as the fire that swept through town in 1879. Mine buildings were the first to blaze as hoist men hurriedly brought miners to the surface. The residents formed bucket brigades and saved some of the buildings in the business district while many of their own homes went up in smoke. Long piles of firewood, carefully stacked and ready for winter, fueled the flames. Discouraged miners and their families moved away. The mines had begun to play out as well.

Horses and automobiles both were in use when this photo of the Caribou shaft house was taken in 1926. Carnegie Branch Library for Local History, Boulder Historical Society Collection.

There was some mining activity in Caribou in the 1880s, but the declining price of silver and the silver crash in 1893 did nothing to revitalize Caribou's fortunes. Many of the miners moved to Central City and Cripple Creek. By 1910, Caribou had only fifty-one people. There was little mining, just a few retired miners who had seen the camp in its glory days and didn't want to move on.

Unlike many other Boulder County mining towns which are now residential communities, Caribou today is a ghost town. All that remains of the once-busy camp are the stone walls from the Potosi Mining Company's office building (built after the fire) and part of one log cabin.

> *To get to Caribou, turn west (left if you're driving north) off the Peak to Peak Highway (Colorado 72) onto County Road 128, just north of Nederland. About a third of the way up the five-mile drive are some sharp switchbacks where the town of Cardinal suddenly grew in 1881.*
>
> *Continue to the end of the "improved" dirt road.*

THE SWITZERLAND TRAIL OF AMERICA

Miners in western Boulder County realized that in order to lower their costs for shipping ore and to bring in coal for their steam-powered machinery, they needed a railroad. Given the mountainous terrain, it would have to be a narrow gauge line. Plans went forward for a railroad with the optimistic name of the Greeley, Salt Lake & Pacific, intending to tap the mining towns and then cross the Continental Divide. In its early years, the railroad succeeded in promoting the local mining industry. It also had an unexpected bonus -- it brought in tourists.

The first Greeley, Salt Lake & Pacific train left Boulder on April 6, 1883 for what was then known as Penn Gulch, a mining camp later renamed Sunset, in Four Mile Canyon. There was no place for the train to turn around, so it simply headed up and then backed down. A wagon road ran from the end of the track to Ward, improving travel between Ward and Boulder.

Early travelers befriended a little bulldog who also rode the train. He'd get on at one stop, get off at another, stay for awhile, then ride the train to another stop. No one knew who owned him or whether he had a home. The trainmen called him Grover Cleveland, after the current President of the United States.

The Greeley, Salt Lake & Pacific had a relatively short life span. This first narrow gauge was washed out in the flood of 1894. For four years there was no way for the miners to ship ore by rail. Then the Colorado & Northwestern Railroad came to the rescue. In 1898, it rebuilt the bridges and track, built a wye at Sunset, and constructed a grade and laid tracks to Ward. The total trackage from Boulder to Ward was twenty-six miles.

Eastern investors behind the railroad had high hopes for its success. A reporter for the *Rocky Mountain News* stated, "In such a small beginning there are great possibilities. It is believed that it is the germ from which will spring another great railroad system. Those who are best acquainted with the capitalists backing this enterprise are confident that they will not be content until the road reaches away out and beyond into Middle Park, to Salt Lake City and eventually to the Pacific coast." Little did anyone realize that David H. Moffat's Denver, Northwestern & Pacific would ultimately accomplish some of what the promoters of the Colorado & Northwestern hoped it would do.

Railroad advertisements stated that "one need not go to Switzerland for sublime mountain scenery." The line offered a cash prize for a name that would bring out the romance and beauty of Boulder County. The contest was won by Professor Snooks for the name "The Switzerland Trail." The words "of America" were added later.

Ladies in long dresses gathered wild flowers during group outings to Mont Alto, a railroad-owned resort between Sunset and the Gold Hill station on the northern branch to Ward. There the Colorado & Northwestern Railroad Company built a picnic pavilion complete with a large stone fireplace. To the west was a twenty-foot basin surrounding a white quartz fountain. Water to both the building and the fountain was piped from a spring 3,000 feet away on the hillside. The company hosted baseball games, dances, concerts, and lectures by University and Chautauqua speakers. Even flatcars loaded with beer on ice were left with the passengers for a carefree day in the mountains. The stone fireplace is all that is left of the pavilion today, although people still stop for picnics. The United States Forest Service has provided tables, barbecue grills, and rest rooms.

Mont Alto was a favorite with excursionists in 1898 after the railroad was extended from Sunset to Ward. Carnegie Branch Library for Local History, Boulder Historical Society Collection.

The Colorado & Northwestern Railroad wasn't without its problems. In 1901, an avalanche at Camp Frances, near Ward, threw the train off the track and killed several men. Fierce snows nearly overcame the line's snowplows and the two hundred men who were hired to shovel snow off the tracks.

The Ward and Eldora branches split at the town of Sunset. Above, the train pulls out of the Sunset station. Below, an artist shows the railroad attaining new heights. Pettem collection.

Meanwhile, Eldora miners opened a promising vein of gold ore in the Mogul Tunnel at Eldora. As a result, the railroad company decided to extend its line twenty miles from Sunset to Eldora. Officials hoped that this southern branch would be the one that would go over the Continental Divide. Construction through the mountains took some time. The first train rolled into Sulphide Flats and then Eldora in January, 1905.

At Glacier Lake, tourists could add boating to their other activities. Pettem collection.

The tracks to Eldora passed Glacier Lake. Always anxious to please its customers, the railroad company moved its entire Mont Alto pavilion to the lake so that patrons could add boating to their other pastimes. The Glacier Lake Pavilion soon became very popular. The largest excursion brought 2,700 people who were crowded into eighteen railroad cars. During the winters, ice from Glacier Lake was cut into two-foot thick blocks and sold to Boulder's Crystal Springs Brewery. Today the lake is privately owned and fenced in, and not even visible from the Peak to Peak Highway.

The years 1905 to 1909 were slow for the railroad. The Mogul Tunnel didn't do as well as expected, and several big mines at Ward shut down. Eventually the Colorado & Northwestern was sold to a new company, the Denver, Boulder & Western, nicknamed the "drink beer and wine" by some of its passengers. Caribou's silver boom had been over before the trains arrived at nearby Cardinal, but the construction of Barker Dam and tungsten mining during the World War provided some business for a while. Summer tourists still piled onto the trains for trips to the mountains, but they also began to travel in motor cars.

Trucks were used, too, to haul ore and supplies. Soon the once-romantic Switzerland Trail of America couldn't meet its expenses or pay its taxes. When a flood washed out many bridges and miles of track in 1919, the railroad's time was over. Track was removed and sold to other railroads in Wyoming, California, and even in Japan. Engine Number 30, later used on the Denver and South Park and on the Rio Grande Southern Railroads, was retired in 1952 to Boulder's Central Park, a "memorial to Colorado railroad and mining pioneers."

Although the trains are gone, segments of the railroad grade are widely used by hikers, bicyclists, cross-country skiers, and four-wheelers. The scenery remains the same.

To reach a section of the southern branch of the railroad grade, turn east (right if you're driving north) from the Peak to Peak Highway (Colorado 72) onto an unmarked dirt road 5.8 miles north of Nederland. Soon on your left you'll pass the locked gate to Glacier Lake where vacationers once could do as they pleased.

The dirt road continues along a ridge for 6 miles until it is near the summit of Sugarloaf Mountain (Sugarloaf station). Then the grade winds and descends for 4 miles into the town of Sunset. From there you can follow Four Mile Canyon (County Road 118) for the 13.8-mile drive to Boulder, or drive part of the northern branch of the Switzerland Trail to its intersection with County Road 52.

To reach a section of the northern branch of the railroad grade, turn east (right if you're driving north) from the Peak to Peak Highway (Colorado 72) onto County Road 52, which is 8.4 miles north of Nederland or 2.8 miles south of Ward. A sign will read "Gold Hill." Follow County Road 52 for 4 miles to Gold Hill station, the closest the railroad got to Gold Hill, and where the railroad once crossed the road. A sign will direct you to the right to reach the Mont Alto picnic ground (in 1 mile) and on down to Sunset (another 2.8 miles). From there you can follow Four Mile Canyon (County Road 118) for the 13.8-mile drive to Boulder, or drive part of the southern branch to Sugarloaf station and back to the Peak to Peak Highway.

Four-wheel drive or high clearance vehicles are recommended.

The Continental Divide provides a scenic backdrop to the town of Gold Hill. Photo by author, 1988.

GOLD HILL

The Pikes Peak gold rush had scarcely begun when members of the Aikins party, who had left Brownsville, Nebraska, in the fall of 1858, found gold in the mountains west of present-day Boulder. When the news reached the Cherry Creek diggings in present-day Denver, hundreds of prospectors rushed to the mountains to pan for gold at what they called "Mountain District Number 1, Nebraska Territory." Gold Hill, the settlement they founded became the first permanent mining town in what is now Colorado.

In the summer of 1859 the miners washed thousands of dollars worth of gold from the stream they named Gold Run. After the placer miners had had their day, the harder task of underground mining began. In June, 1860, David Horsfal discovered the Horsfal mine, Gold Hill's most famous and productive early property. Until 1865, the gold from this mine supported both Gold Hill and its supply town of Boulder.

As rich as the deposits were, the techniques used to process the ores were inadequate. As a result, most hard rock mining in Boulder County wasn't profitable in the 1860s. Miners left to fight in the Civil War, take up farming, or try their luck in the newly-discovered gold mines of Montana.

In 1872, the assay of an unfamiliar ore revealed that it contained tellurium in combination with gold and silver. It was said that pieces of rock that appeared to have no precious metals were in fact so rich that roasting them on top of a wood stove would bring out the pure gold in bubbles. This prompted a second gold rush to western Boulder County.

Prospectors spread out from Gold Hill and discovered gold-tellurides in surrounding areas. Some knew what to look for and others were just lucky. In 1875, Henry Meyring discovered the Melvina mine near Salina. The newly-arrived German carpenter asked some experienced miners where he might find some gold. Knowing him as a tenderfoot, the miners jokingly told him to dig in the shade of the biggest tree on top of the hill. He did, and made over eight thousand dollars within two weeks. The Melvina mine became one of the largest in the area.

Social activity in Gold Hill centered around the Wentworth Hotel, built in 1873. Poet Eugene Field, then working for the *Denver Tribune,* was a frequent visitor. He commemorated the hotel with the poem, "Casey's Table D'Hote." In later years, attorney Clarence Darrow was also reported to have spent part of his summers there.

In 1921, the Wentworth Hotel was purchased by the Holiday House Association and became the Blue Bird Lodge. Its purpose was to accommodate the "Blue Birds," who were vacationing young businesswomen from Chicago. It was reported by one of them that they had found a place where "winds will blow their own freshness into you and the storms their energy while cares will drop off like autumn leaves."

The porch and dormers were added to the hotel at this time, and the clapboard siding was removed to expose the building's log structure. A dining room built next door in 1926 is now the Gold Hill Inn Restaurant.

Above, the Blue Bird Lodge in the 1920s with the town well in the foreground. Carnegie Branch Library for Local History, Boulder Historical Society Collection. Today the building is the same and the well is still there. Photo by author, 1996.

The Gold Hill Store is one of the buildings in the Gold Hill Historic District. Photo by author, 1977.

Other Gold Hill tourists stayed at the Double M Ranch which later became the Trojan Ranch Summer Camp. A number of the miners' cabins were sold as summer residences to vacationers who came year after year.

Gold mining at the time had gone into another slump until the Roosevelt Administration, during the Depression, raised the price of gold from $20.67 to $35.00 an ounce. That prompted another mining revival. Mines like the Slide, Cold Spring, Red Cloud, Alamakee, and St. Joe were reworked for low grade ore previously found unprofitable. Then, in 1942, the mines closed again as gold was not essential for World War II.

Gold Hill is now a quiet residential community. Its oldest buildings date from the 1870s, giving the town the feel of an earlier era. Besides pioneer log and early wood frame homes and commercial buildings, a few decorative Victorian homes provide evidence of Gold Hill's evolution from an early mining camp to a permanent town.

In 1989, forty-seven buildings were formed into the Gold Hill Historic District and placed on the National Register of Historic Places. Because the rural character of the town has been maintained and only minimal changes have been made to many of its buildings, Gold Hill is considered the best intact representation of all of Boulder County's precious metal mining communities. There are a few stores, a restaurant, and the two-room schoolhouse, built in 1895, still in session.

Just off County Road 52, between Gold Hill and Boulder, is the school built to serve the mining community of Sunshine. Unlike other one-room mountain schools, this one is built of stone, and is also listed on the National Register of Historic Places.

The Sunshine School. Courtesy Jeanne Elizer.

> To reach Gold Hill, turn east (right if you're driving north) from the Peak to Peak Highway (Colorado 72) onto County Road 52, which is 8.4 miles north of Nederland. Follow the dirt road east along a ridge. In 4 miles you'll pass the site of Gold Hill station, a stop on the Switzerland Trail. In 3 more miles you'll come to Gold Hill itself.
>
> To get to Sunshine, stay on County Road 52 (straight through Gold Hill). The road climbs uphill for a short distance before it descends into Boulder. In 4 miles, after an extended section of dirt road (just before the road permanently turns to pavement), is a turn-off to the left to Sunshine. The school will be just around the bend on your left.

WARD

The town of Ward dates from the spring of 1860 when a miner named Calvin Ward located a claim he called the Miser's Dream. More prospectors rushed to the area and opened a number of other gold mines.

As underground work progressed, the miners began to demand the construction of stamp mills to crush the ore and free the gold. Teamsters used hundreds of oxen to pull wagon loads of machinery across the plains and up a primitive wagon road in Left Hand Canyon. However, most of Ward's trade in the early days was with Black Hawk. The route through present-day Nederland became today's Peak to Peak Highway.

In 1867, a reporter wrote of "good-class frame houses, and one water-powered and five steam-powered stamp mills." He described the typical miner as "taking comfort in eating his slapjacks and sow-belly, garnished with a dessert of dried apples, hopefully awaiting the day when a fortune would jump into his lap from between walls of rock."

Another reporter, in 1892, described the people of Ward as "prosperous, enterprising, and hospitable." They had a weekly newspaper, a fifteen-piece band, and a good school. A stagecoach made two trips daily from Sunset, the first terminus of the Switzerland Trail.

Ward's most famous citizens were Horace Tabor and his wife Baby Doe, along with their daughters Lily and Silver

Dollar. Tabor had been in Colorado since the initial gold rush. He had made an immense fortune at Leadville in the late 1870s and early 1880s, went on to a scandalous divorce from his first wife Augusta, and then, as a United States senator, married the young glamorous Baby Doe with President Chester A. Arthur in attendance.

 Horace and Baby Doe had lived in extravagance, and Horace made too many lavish public benefactions and bad investments. By the early 1890s, he had overextended himself, and the silver crash of 1893 destroyed what remained of his fortune. After losing everything, 67 year-old Tabor got a loan from Winfield Scott Stratton (who struck it rich in gold in Cripple Creek) and turned to Ward where he worked the Eclipse mine north of town from 1897 to 1898 in hopes of reclaiming his wealth.

 Fortune did not smile on Tabor again, After a year at Ward, Tabor's friends got President McKinley to appoint him postmaster of Denver, where he lived comfortably again, but only to die of appendicitis a year later. Daughter Lily went to Wisconsin to live with her mother's relatives. Silver Dollar moved to Chicago where she lived in a series of flophouses and died under mysterious circumstances. The penniless Baby Doe went back to Leadville where she lived in abject poverty in a shack at the Matchless mine until she died in 1935.

 Tabor had probably gone to Ward too soon. Although he and his small crew didn't find much ore in the Eclipse, the town exploded into activity once the railroad arrived in 1898. Governor Alva Adams rode in the first of nine coaches. The train stopped along the way so a band could play "The Star Spangled Banner." Wrote one journalist along for the ride, "Old Glory floated proudly from a giant pine." When the train reached

Ward, there was a thirteen-gun salute, and "the hills echoed and re-echoed with a hundred thousand cheers." Someone claimed that there were more flags than required by an ordinary navy.

By 1900, homes and businesses were tightly packed into the mountain valley. On January 24, about one o'clock in the morning, Mrs. M. J. McClancy, the owner of the Hotel McClancy, discovered a fire in an ashcan next to the building. "Had she a bucket of water handy," wrote a reporter, "it could have been easily extinguished, but before she could hunt up a bucket and pump it full of water, the flames had gained such headway that her bucket was useless. The wind was blowing a gale, and the flames soon swept across the street and the city was doomed. With neither water works nor a fire company, the people became desperate. Nothing could be done but try to save the furniture and goods."

Fifty-two mine whistles sounded the alarm. Women and children huddled on the hillsides as the fire burned unchecked for six hours. It was unseasonably warm, as a Chinook wind of hurricane force pushed down from the Continental Divide. Attempts to extinguish the fire were futile until a rare shift in the wind came with the first light of dawn. For a few seconds, the flames shot straight up, then retreated over the area already burned.

Ward was a disaster. Few businesses had escaped destruction. Townsfolk had spent the night drenching the schoolhouse and the Congregational Church with buckets of water and wet blankets and quilts. These two landmarks saved the residential sections behind them, and are still part of Ward today. Both are duly recorded on the National Register of Historic Places. Today the school building houses the town hall, library, and post office.

This 1910 view of Ward shows the Congregational Church (center), the railroad depot (upper right), and the Columbia Hotel (foreground). Photo by Ed Tangen. Carnegie Branch Library for Local History, Boulder Historical Society Collection.

The Congregational (Community) Church, Columbia Hotel, and depot are still in Ward. The depot has been moved to the uphill side of the grade. Photo by author, 1988.

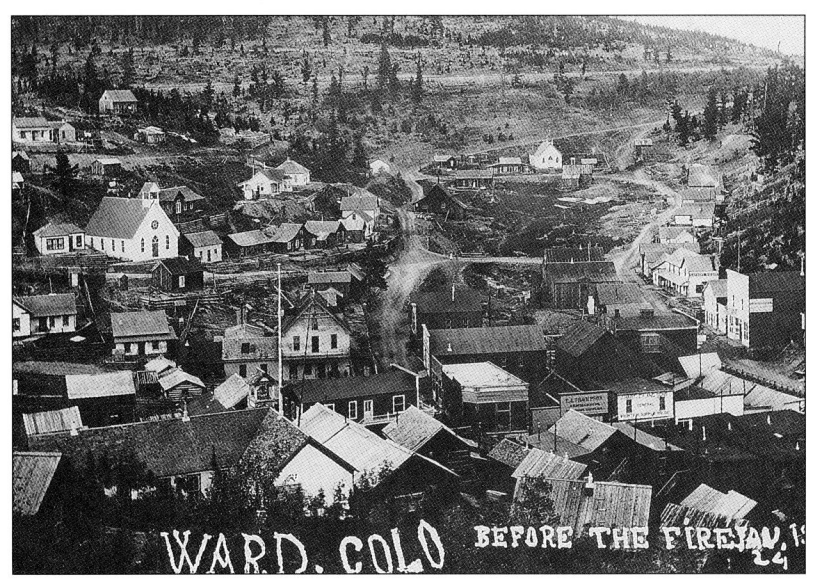

Ward before the 1900 fire, and as it is today. The church looks the same. Above, Carnegie Branch Library for Local History, Boulder. Below, photo by Clara Pettem, 1996.

After the fire, a newspaper editorial expressed the sentiments in town. "We're still here. Disfigured badly, of course, but you can't drown the *Miner*. We expect to stay in Ward."

Much of Ward was enthusiastically rebuilt of sturdier materials. In 1904, it became the largest mining town in Boulder County. The biggest producer was the Big Five Company which employed one hundred men in its "million-dollar properties" -- the Adit, Columbia, Dew-Drop, and Niwot mines.

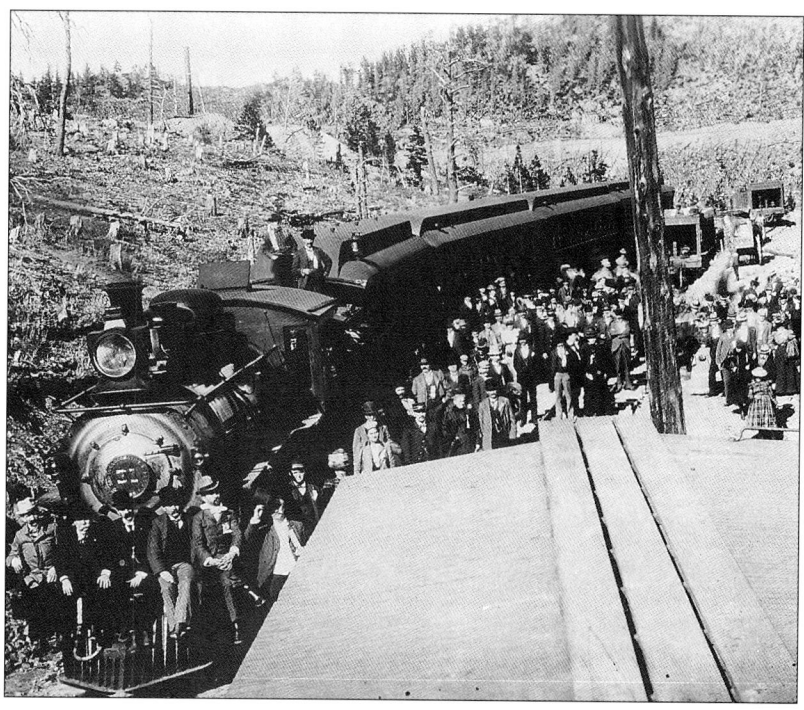

Tourists, many of them from Chautauqua, in Boulder, took the train to Ward and nearby Camp Frances where "even the ladies" toured an underground gold mine. Pettem collection.

At this time, the town was also beginning to shift to a tourist economy. As the northern terminus of the Switzerland Trail, Ward became the jumping off point for Stapp's Lake Lodge and other resorts between Ward and Estes Park. When Rocky Mountain National Park opened in 1915, tourists arrived in Ward on the train, then transferred to Stanley Steamer Mountain Wagons.

After the railroad was abandoned and all tourists came by automobile, Ward served passing motorists and acted as the official post office for neighboring resorts. In the 1960s, the town accommodated an influx of hippies besides its few old timers. Today's section of the Peak to Peak Highway intersects with County Road 106 but bypasses the town of Ward.

BRAINARD LAKE AND PEACEFUL VALLEY

The most spectacular view of the Indian Peaks Wilderness Area accessible by car is from Brainard Lake, just 5 miles from the Peak to Peak Highway. At 10,300 feet, the area offers camping, fishing, and hiking, and, in winter, plenty of cross-country skiing.

The wilderness area of nearly 75,000-acres lies in two counties. The eastern part is in Roosevelt National Forest in Boulder County, and the western part is in Arapaho National Forest in Grand County. Many of the peaks are more than 12,000 feet high, and are a favorite with hikers and climbers.

Brainard Lake, just one of many glacier-made lakes in the area, was once the water source for the Utica Mining, Milling, and Reservoir Company which patented the lake and the immediate surrounding area in 1898. Eventually the lake and surrounding land was sold to the United States Forest Service which now maintains it for public use. A small fee is charged for admission.

At the surrounding parking lots are trail heads for Mitchell, Blue, Long, and Isabelle lakes, as well as Mount Audubon and other peaks, Pawnee Pass, and the Isabelle and Fair Glaciers. Many hikes are suitable for families, even those with small children. To fully enjoy the Indian Peaks, be sure you're well-equipped and prepared for sudden changes in temperature and weather.

Brainard Lake is a good place to see the Indian Peaks. For a closer look, there are numerous hiking trails. Courtesy Daily Camera.

If you hike above Brainard Lake, you'll reach timberline at approximately 11,500 feet. Above that is the alpine zone with its fragile ecosystem due to the severe cold in winter, the strong winds, and the short growing season in summer. Dwarf willow and spruce hug the ground. Marsh marigolds, Parry primroses, and moss campion bloom as soon as the snow begins to melt, which can be as late as July or early August. Pikas, which look like guinea pigs, make high-pitched whistling calls and scurry across rocky slopes.

Even if you don't get out of your car, Brainard Lake is well worth the short drive from the highway.

> *To get to Brainard Lake, turn west (left if you're driving north) off the Peak to Peak Highway (Colorado 72), onto County Road 102 just north of Ward. In 2.5 miles, half way to Brainard Lake, is Red Rock Lake, a beautiful lake and a favorite with fishermen. The road is only open to this point in winter.*

Red Rock Lake is on the way to Brainard Lake, only a short drive off the Peak to Peak Highway. Photo by Ed Raines, 1988.

Stagecoach travelers who continued north from the Ward area in the early days often stopped at a homesteaded cabin called Wildcat Gulch. In 1908, John and Mildred Roberts purchased the property, renamed it Peaceful Valley, and started a resort.

Roberts called Peaceful Valley "an ideal family summer resort of 320 acres." Some of its features included "good river fishing and near lake fishing, its scenery cannot be excelled, livery of gentle animals, the best of sanitary precautions, and a day nursery permitting mothers to rest and to take proper outing." Peaceful Valley was advertised as "a place to rest, free from style and stiffness. Ladies go in overalls. You can be one of the big family out for a good time, or you can keep by yourself and your study."

Amusements included tennis, croquet, quoits, hikes, horseback riding, dancing, musical evenings, and swings and merry-go-rounds for children. Not permitted, according to rumored accounts in later years, were drinking, gambling, and card playing. It was said that Roberts would look in the windows at his guests and throw out anyone who participated in these activities.

When glaciers were on everyone's minds, Peaceful Valley was advertised as the gateway to the Middle St. Vrain Glacier. Wagons, stagecoaches, and, later, Stanley Steamers met incoming guests who arrived on the train in Ward. Peaceful Valley became a regular stop for all public, and most private, transportation between Ward and Estes Park. An added attraction was the newly-established post office at the Peaceful Valley store. Groceries were stocked for campers, as well as gasoline, oil, and grease for the motorist.

These guests stopped at Peaceful Valley's combination store, post office, and gas station, ca. 1930s. Carnegie Branch Library for Local History, Boulder.

The resort's specialty in the mid-1920s was "serving dinners to auto parties" with "the best meal for the money to be found in the hills." Cabins rented for eleven to fourteen dollars per week.

Roberts may not have charged enough, as he soon lost his property by foreclosure. In 1928, Peaceful Valley was reopened under new management as the Forest Inn Hotel. After a couple more changes in ownership, the resort was purchased in 1953 by Karl and Mabel Boehm who built the struggling business into the Peaceful Valley Lodge and Guest Ranch.

The present resort continues to offer its guests hiking, fishing, and pack trips, along with a chance to rest in an unhurried mountain setting. The alpine chapel, built in 1977 as a memorial to Paul F. Boehm, Karl Boehm's father, is popular for weddings. The onion-shaped dome reflects his Austrian heritage.

Peaceful Valley is a short turn-off from the Peak to Peak Highway at the bottom of the hill between Ward and the Middle St. Vrain Canyon. Look back to see the chapel high above on the mountainside.

Peaceful Valley chapel. Photo by author, 1993.

ALLENSPARK AREA

Tourists in the late teens and early 1920s climbed the Highline/Skyline Road (County Road 105 and 105J) to reach the Allenspark area. By the mid-1920s, the lower road was improved and the Highline/Skyline Road was rarely used.

Northbound travelers from Peaceful Valley followed the creek to the town of Raymond where they could find a room or good meal at the Raymonds Hotel. Motorists then began the long uphill climb to Allenspark. County Road 103 still goes through the Peaceful Valley and Raymond communities. However, today's Peak to Peak Highway cuts into the mountainside just after the Raymond turn-off and gains elevation before Colorado 72 comes to its junction with Colorado 7.

A left turn (if you're driving north) at this junction leads to Ferncliff, Allenspark, Copeland Lake, Meeker Park, the Longs Peak trail head, and Estes Park. To the right is South Saint Vrain Canyon which runs down to Lyons (see Boulder Loop Tour).

Alonzo N. Allen was among the first to homestead land east of the present community named for him. The first schoolhouse in the area was the Bunce School, built ca. 1888. Today it's little changed, but empty, and is on the National Register of Historic Places. It is the best-preserved log schoolhouse in Boulder County.

The Bunce School near Allenspark. Photo by author, 1996.

By the turn of the twentieth century, Allenspark was a favorite tent camping spot for visitors from Longmont and nearby communities. The people would run cattle, cut hay, or just vacation while escaping the heat of the plains.

Allenspark is at the very northeastern end of Colorado's mineral belt. Although thirty-three gold mines were patented in the mining district, the area was not well-mineralized. Appropriately-named claims like the Overdraft, Perseverance, and the Hard Money produced little ore.

Tourism took over the Allenspark's economy earlier than in most other mining towns. The "Allen's Park Commercial Club" formed in 1920 "for the purpose of letting the world know of the charm of this beautiful resort." Well-known at the time was the Crystal Springs Lodge and other resorts and guest ranches. Will's Resort, another of the early ones, evolved into

Presbyterian Highlands Ranch. The Allenspark Lodge, built in 1933, is now a bed and breakfast.

The Allenspark Lodge features rustic architecture. Photo by author, 1996.

The Allenspark Community Church is a log building with stained glass windows of native wild flowers. Services are interdenominational and vacationers are welcome, even in their hiking clothes.

The nearby town of Ferncliff also competed for the tourist trade. Both towns were bypassed in the 1958 rerouting of the Peak to Peak Highway. Nearby, a scenic overlook gives an uninterrupted view of 13,911-foot Mount Meeker.

North of Allenspark is a turn-off to the west (left if you're driving north) to Wild Basin. After you turn you'll pass Copeland Lake, now popular with fishermen. In the early days it was the location of the Copeland Lake Lodge which later became the Wild Basin Lodge and burned in 1980. A section of the "old" road (County Road 84W) extends south of Copeland Lake to the Olive Ridge campground before it connects with today's highway.

The dirt road (County Road 115) to Wild Basin ends at a Ranger Station within Rocky Mountain National Park. Unlike the main section of the park, there is no fee to enter. Trail heads begin there for a number of outstanding hikes. In the summer biweekly flower identification walks are given by the forest rangers.

Keith Dever, whose parents built the Meeker Park Lodge, stands on the porch of his lodge. Photo by author, 1996.

Back on the Peak to Peak Highway and on your right (driving north) is Meeker Park. The Dever family started construction on the Meeker Park Lodge in 1930. Adjoining lots were sold to friends who built primitive cabins which eventually became modernized rental cabins. Many of the same guests return year after year making up an extended "Meeker Park family." Today the lodge is still run by the same family.

Further north, on the left, is Camp Saint Milo. In 1916, a Denver priest selected the site as a summer camp for choir boys. The location centered around a large rock on which he intended to build their church. The camp was established in 1921. Soon afterwards, the priest found out that his rock was in the path of Peak to Peak Highway improvements. After extended discussions with the governor and even federal officials, the rock was not dynamited as planned. Instead the road was routed around the rock.

Saint Catherine's Chapel was the dream of a Catholic priest many years ago. Photo by author, 1996.

Saint Catherine's Chapel was built on the rock in 1936. Today Camp Saint Milo and the chapel are owned by the Denver Archdiocese. A modern building on the camp property is now used as a convention center.

Continuing north, on the right, is a combination store and museum called Eagle Plume's. In the 1920s, the business was Perkins Trading Post which sold mostly antiques. With the help of Charles Eagle Plume, the owners shifted the focus of their shop to the arts and crafts of the American Indian. The late Eagle Plume was a noted lecturer on Indian art and culture, and included Chautauqua, in Boulder, on his speaking circuit.

Shortly on the left is the trail head to 14,255-foot Longs Peak, the highest point in Rocky Mountain National Park. The mountain takes its name from Major Stephen H. Long who led an army expedition to the foot of the Rockies in 1820. Interest in climbing the peak rose dramatically in the 1860s. In 1866, science-fiction writer Jules Verne wrote *From Earth to Moon* in which he envisioned a 280-foot telescope with a sixteen-foot reflector on the mountain's summit to track an imagined moon shot from Florida.

Two years after Verne's work, William N. Byers, the editor of *Rocky Mountain News,* and Major John Wesley Powell, the one-armed United States Geological Survey chief, made the first known ascent. In 1914, however, an elderly Arapaho related the story that his father, Old Man Gunn, had reached the summit earlier to trap eagles for feathers. Old Man Gunn was said to have taken a stuffed coyote for bait, hid in a covered pit, and seized the eagles by their feet when they landed on the carcass.

The first woman to climb the peak was Addie Alexander. She was followed by Anna Dickinson and Isabella Bird, an

Englishwoman who later wrote that she was "dragged, like a bale of goods" up the mountain.

Longs Peak, with its flat top, as seen from Mount Audubon. Pettem collection.

Isabella Bird summed up her climb by writing, "It was something at last to stand upon the stormrent crown of this lonely sentinel of the Rocky Range, on one of the mightiest of the vertebrae of the backbone of the North American continent, and to see the waters start for both oceans. Uplifted above love and hate and storms of passion, calm amidst the eternal silences, fanned by zephyrs and bathed in living blue, peace rested for that one bright day on the Peak."

These early tourists, at Sheep's Head Rock, are on their way up South Saint Vrain Canyon. Carnegie Branch Library for Local History, Boulder.

ESTES PARK

When the Stanley Steamers transported tourists between Ward and the town of Estes Park, they regularly stopped at the Longs Peak Inn, the Columbines, and the Hewes-Kirkwood Inn, all approximately nine miles south of Estes Park. The three resorts were convenient starting-off points for climbers to reach the summit of Longs Peak.

Naturalist Enos Mills made nearly three hundred ascents. Mills grew up in Kansas, but felt what he called "the spell of the wilds," and, in 1885, homesteaded literally in the shadow of Longs Peak. As you continue north on the Peak to Peak Highway, look on your right for a historical marker placed by the Daughters of the American Revolution. It states, "Enos A. Mills. Father of the Rocky Mountain National Park, internationally known naturalist, author, lecturer, and nature guide, homesteaded on this site 1885."

The homestead cabin, which was placed on the National Register of Historic Places in 1973, is visible across a meadow in the trees. During the summer months, drive in to be personally guided through the cabin by a member of the family. Inside is a collection of Mills's books and photographs. On a board hanging next to the doorway is the inscription, "This is a beautiful world, and all who go out under the open sky will feel the gentle influence of nature."

The Enos Mills homestead cabin is to the left in the trees behind the historical marker next to the road. Photo by author, 1996.

Mills also was an innkeeper and built the original Longs Peak Inn (which burned down in 1949) on the other side of the road. As development increased, Mills envisioned the creation of a Rocky Mountain National Park which would extend from the Wyoming border south to Pikes Peak. His writings and lecture tours did much to familiarize the American people with the great natural beauty of the region. Year after year he pushed for and finally achieved the Park's creation but had to settle for the smaller area around Estes Park.

After the Rocky Mountain National Park first opened in 1915, there was demand for additional hotels and lodges. In 1917, the Baldpate Inn was built two miles down the road. The rustic inn was named for the novel *Seven Keys to Baldpate* in which seven people each believed they held the only key to an isolated mountain hotel. Guests have been donating keys ever since, and the hotel boasts the largest collection of keys in the world. The Baldpate Inn, on the National Register of Historic Places, is on a section of the "old" road to the east of today's Peak to Peak Highway just before it descends into Estes Park.

Unlike the mining towns from the Central City area through Allenspark, Estes Park had no paying quantities of minerals. Instead the town's economy has almost always centered on tourism. It was named for early rancher Joel Estes who got discouraged and moved away in 1866 after six rugged years of cattle raising.

In the 1870s, when there were only a handful of people in the area, early settler W. E. James built the Elkhorn Lodge. It has been enlarged and modernized, but the public rooms feature a collection of massive elk trophies and some of the original furnishings. In 1877, Lord Dunraven, who encouraged his friends to come and hunt, built the luxurious fifty-room English Hotel. It was destroyed by fire in 1911. One of Dunraven's guests was artist Albert Bierstadt, whose paintings of the Estes Park region spread its fame all over the world.

Meanwhile, F. O. Stanley, 54 years old and suffering from tuberculosis, moved from Massachusetts to Estes Park to try to improve his health. He bought over six thousand acres of land from Lord Dunraven and built the large and elegant Stanley Hotel which opened in 1909. Stanley, who always enjoyed a prank, arranged to have stuffed but realistic bears jump out and scare his guests as they were driven from one of the railroad terminals. The Stanley Hotel is one of several remaining historic properties in Estes Park.

The Rocky Mountain Transportation Company's bright red open buses replaced some of the Stanley Steamer Mountain Wagons in 1916. Tourists in their own automobiles and others in the buses rode up to the Continental Divide on the park's Fall River Road when it opened in 1920. Soon so many motorists were negotiating the steep narrow road and sharp switchbacks that there was a need for a new road. Trail Ridge Road, which reaches 12,183 feet, was completed in 1932. It continues on to Granby and U.S. 40, and is the highest continuous automobile highway in the United States.

Trail Ridge Road, ca. 1930s. Pettem collection.

After Trail Ridge Road opened, the Fall River Road was used only for one-way traffic, as it is today. Additional information on Rocky Mountain National Park can be obtained at the Estes Park visitor center at the junction of Colorado 7 and U.S. 34 (to Loveland). Also, be sure to see the historical exhibits at the Estes Park Historical Museum on the corner of 4th Street and U.S. 36 (to Lyons).

PART III

BOULDER LOOP TOUR

This 72.6-mile tour through some of the most beautiful country in Boulder County is all on paved roads. Plan a few stops along the way and turn it into a half-day outing.

This Boulder Loop Tour begins in Nederland, then follows the Peak to Peak Highway (Colorado 72) to Colorado 7, goes down the South Saint Vrain Canyon to Lyons, goes to Boulder on the North Foothills Highway (U.S. 36), and returns to Nederland via Boulder Canyon (Colorado 119). However, the loop can be started anywhere along the tour and go in either direction.

The 22.3-mile drive from Nederland to Colorado 7 has been covered in the chapters on Nederland, Caribou, the Switzerland Trail, Gold Hill, Ward, and Brainard Lake and Peaceful Valley. If you haven't had a chance to detour to Brainard Lake (5 miles from the Peak to Peak Highway), it's worth the time to do so. No other paved road will take you to such a spectacular view of the Indian Peaks. Take the left turn onto County Road 102 just north of Ward (12 miles north of Nederland).

SOUTH SAINT VRAIN CANYON

In a little over 10 miles from the Brainard Lake turn-off, Colorado 72 will intersect with Colorado 7. Turn right on Colorado 7 to follow the South Saint Vrain Canyon to Lyons. There are numerous picnic spots along the 14.2-mile route.

Named for early fur trader Ceran Saint Vrain, the South Saint Vrain Canyon is known for its rock formations. Promotional literature called it a "craggy fairyland" with formations "that are so perfect they offer no strain to the imagination -- the Indian and his Squaw, the Barking Dog, Elephant Rock, Napoleon Rock, The Old Woman of the Mountain, and the Natural Fireplace." Another writer stated, "The South Saint Vrain has only one crop to offer the nation -- and mighty proud about it -- its scenery."

Between 1890 and ca. 1910, all travelers had to stop and pay a toll near the mouth of the canyon. Teamsters were charged per horse and were known to have unhitched two of their four horses in order to lead them up and around the toll gates instead of passing through with their wagons.

LYONS

After you come into Lyons and cross the North Saint Vrain Creek, turn right onto Colorado 7, Colorado 66, and U. S. 36. On your right will be the railroad depot (now the Lyons Depot Library) built in the mid-1880s when the Denver, Utah & Pacific Railroad first pulled into town. The depot closed in 1960, then was purchased by the town in 1974 during the formation of the Lyons Historical Society. Just to the east, in Sandstone Park, is the Lyons Visitor Center.

The Lyons Depot is now the town's library. Photo by Clara Pettem, 1996.

The depot is one of fifteen sandstone commercial, residential, and public structures in Lyons which have been placed on the National Register of Historic Places. One is the Lyons School on the northeast corner of 4th and High Streets. The one-story stone school was built in 1881, but soon became overcrowded. Additions were made in 1895 and 1902 until it became the present two-story building. Now the building houses the Redstone Museum, open daily June through October.

Lyons was settled in 1880 by Edward S. Lyon, who, like F. O. Stanley, came from the East for his health. As soon as Lyon saw the red sandstone cliffs he recognized the potential for a stone quarry. Soon the town became known for its sandstone, with the first loads hauled in horse-drawn wagons to the railroad in Longmont for shipment to Denver.

Eventually Lyons sandstone, along with stone of varying colors from other quarries located between Boulder and Loveland, became a widely-used building material. In the Lyons area, the stone is red, but further up the Front Range it becomes pink and then buff. Often stone was obtained from several quarries in order to create a blend of colors. Sandstone also was in demand as flagstone for sidewalks and gutters. The Stone Mountain Railroad was built especially to serve the Beach Hill and Noland quarries over the hogback to the east of town.

Lyons sandstone is still in demand and quarried today. The town is also known for its antique shops. Follow Colorado 7, Colorado 66, and U.S. 36 for 1.6 miles east out of Lyons, then turn right and follow the North Foothills Highway (Colorado 7 and U.S. 36) to Boulder.

BOULDER

About half way to Boulder you'll pass the turn-off to Ward via Left Hand Canyon. To continue on this tour, however, keep driving south, then turn right onto Broadway (Colorado 7) as you come into Boulder, 14.5 miles from the beginning of the North Foothills Highway. Follow Broadway for 3.5 miles to Canyon Boulevard and, to follow this tour, turn right to go up Boulder Canyon.

In 1926, the City of Boulder established several auto camps. One was near the mouth of Boulder Canyon. The free campground, now Eben G. Fine Park, provided visiting motorists with electric lights, gas stoves, water, toilets, and laundry and bathing facilities. Accommodations aren't free anymore, but there is much to see and do in Boulder. The Boulder Chamber of Commerce, at Pearl and Folsom Streets, has maps and other tourist information. Visit the Boulder Museum of History on the corner of 12th Street and Euclid Avenue, as well as some of Boulder's historic districts. Stop in at Historic Boulder, Inc. at 646 Pearl Street for a schedule of their walking tours.

The Boulder Downtown Historic District includes many of the buildings on and around the Pearl Street Mall, the early commercial section of the city. Also go see Boulder's Carnegie Library, just west of Broadway at 1125 Pine Street. This Boulder history reference library contains over 200,000 historical photographs and an extensive collection of books and documents on Boulder County. A block away is the beginning of the Mapleton Hill Historic District with some of Boulder's most interesting and historic homes.

The Hale Scientific Building now houses the anthropology department at the University of Colorado. Pettem collection.

Continuing south on Broadway will take you to the campus of the University of Colorado. There you'll see the earliest buildings of the University in the Norlin Quadrangle Historic District. Old Main, the first of the buildings, opened its doors in September, 1877. Visit the University's museum, the Heritage Center, on its third floor.

Other early buildings include Cottage Number 1, Hale Scientific, the President's House (now Koenig Alumni Center), and Woodbury Hall. They all reflect various styles of architecture and building materials. In contrast is Norlin Library, at the east end of the quadrangle. It was completed in 1939, and is a good example of the University's change of architectural style and increased use of sandstone.

The Chautauqua Auditorium was the first building in Boulder to be placed on the National Register of Historic Places. Peter Pollock collection.

Take 13th Street to Baseline Road and turn right to reach the entrance of Chautauqua Park. The community was founded in 1898 as a combination resort and summer school offering classes, cultural programs, and entertainment. The tents of the early days were replaced by cottages which have often stayed in the same families for generations. Chautauqua now offers year-round programs. The Dining Hall is open all summer, and the 1,200-seat auditorium is the home of the Colorado Music Festival.

BOULDER CANYON

Return to Canyon Boulevard (Colorado 119) to continue the Boulder Loop Tour up Boulder Canyon. In 16.5 miles you'll be back in Nederland.

The first road up Boulder Canyon, from the Magnolia turn-off, was completed in 1871 during the silver strike at Caribou. Like South Saint Vrain Canyon, anyone traveling Boulder Canyon in the early days had to pay a toll. Teamsters complained of the high fees and low maintenance, but author Helen Hunt Jackson, an early Boulder tourist who rode down the canyon on horseback in 1878 praised its beauty. She wrote,

"Its gray stone walls rise up, fortress-like from the meadow -- the left hand wall bare and gray, the right hand one thick set with fir from base to top. It is a picture of vivid contrasts -- the green meadow with ranks upon ranks of yellow and red willow bushes making belts of bright color upon it, [and] between the yellows and reds, gleams of white foam flashing, and beyond the high buttress fronts of the canyon mouth, adorned with evergreens."

Buggies and stagecoaches crossed the stream in Boulder Canyon thirty-three times ca. 1900. Carnegie Branch Library for Local History, Boulder Historical Society Collection.

This view looking east in Boulder Canyon below Four Mile Canyon shows the much-improved road after it was rebuilt in the teens. The railroad was on the north side of the canyon. Courtesy Daily Camera.

As late as 1906, the road up Boulder Canyon was still a one-track dirt road. Uphill traffic had the right of way. Teamsters put bells on their horses' harnesses so that approaching traffic would hear them and stop in one of the turnouts. With the automobile came the demand for better roads.

In 1912, a Stanley Steamer was the first automobile to have enough power to pull the steep grade above the narrows in Boulder Canyon. By 1915, during the busy tungsten mining era, twelve-passenger Stanley Steamer Mountain Wagons quietly chugged up the canyon, although horse-drawn stagecoaches continued to transport over a hundred passengers a day.

Meanwhile, the canyon road got much-needed improvements. For four years, beginning in 1913, convicts from the Colorado State Penitentiary in Canon City were hard at work in Boulder Canyon widening and straightening the road and improving the grade. Many of the early bridges were eliminated, and iron culverts replaced those of rotten wood. The road was, for the first time, "double-tracked," and surfaced with crushed rock.

Between 1883 and 1919, the narrow gauge railroad which came to be called the Switzerland Trail ran up Boulder Canyon to its turn-off at Four Mile Canyon. Today some of the railroad grade is a bicycle path and is easily-visible across the creek as you drive up the first mile of the canyon.

Soon you'll go through a tunnel, bored in 1952, which bypasses the Hydroelectric Plant built in 1910. Shortly afterwards will be the turn-off to Magnolia, on your left, and the turn-off to Sugarloaf, on your right. At 8.8 miles from Boulder will be Boulder Falls. The parking lot will be on your left, and the falls on your right, only a short walk from the road.

Boulder Falls was a popular destination point for hikers, horseback riders, and motorists. Courtesy Daily Camera.

The Perfect Tree was another attraction for early-day tourists. It eventually died and fell to the ground. Pettem collection.

Boulder Falls is worth the stop but may have been overrated by early guidebooks. One stated, "The first view of the falls is calculated to make the lover of nature shout in an ecstasy of delight, or in a more thoughtful mood, bow his head in reverent awe in the presence of a scene so wildly grand." Boulderites often took carriage drives, rode horseback, or hiked there for picnics.

In the mid-teens, the waterfall became a destination for members of the Rocky Mountain Climbers Club who traveled from Boulder to Boulder Falls in "two big autos." They explored nearby tungsten mines, then at noon feasted on "beefsteak, aromatic coffee, and accompanying delicacies." They got their exercise by hiking back to Boulder.

After the falls you'll enter the "narrows" where the canyon's rock walls are, obviously, close together. Further up the canyon, and no longer standing, was the Perfect Tree, so named because the spruce was large and well-formed. It, too, became a destination for tourists and others enjoying a day in the mountains. Past the site of the Perfect Tree is Castle Rock, a distinctive rock formation on the left that's popular today with rock climbers.

In 1926, tour promoter Fred Fair, whose Glacier Route Automobile line was transporting tourists up the canyon by the bus load, wrote the following account of "A drive up Boulder Canon [original spelling]" --

"Leaving Boulder, we immediately enter Boulder Canon, famed for its wild and varied scenic beauty. The road winds and twists by a noisy mountain stream, past beautiful Boulder Falls, ever upward between rocks and towering cliffs -- between canon walls so narrow that it seems as though the water itself would engulf the car.

Suddenly we emerge from the turn in the wall and we realize that it was but a plunge in fancy, for the road climbs as rapidly as the grade of the stream, and though dwarfed by comparison with the awful rock masses towering a thousand feet above, it is wide and safe for travel."

"From the gorge we suddenly emerge into a beautiful valley, the land of the perfect pine, only to be again swallowed up by the canon depths, with Castle Rock silently guarding their eternal entrance. Passing this sentinel of a million years, we enter the path of an extinct giant river of ice that flowed when the range was young, and a remnant of which Arapahoe [Arapaho] Glacier alone remains."

"As the road climbs higher and higher along the mountainside, one begins to feel the cool breezes from the land of everlasting snow, and as we round the sharp turn of Barker Dam there suddenly breaks into view a picture so beautiful, in all its majesty and awe-inspiring splendor, as to defy language and art to describe it -- the Rocky Mountains with their eternal snow-capped peaks made doubly impressive by their mirrored reflection in Nederland Lake, and the little city upon its western shore."

Fair's description leaves us in Nederland, where this loop tour began. But for those who want to keep driving, he continued, "From Nederland the road winds and climbs among smooth hills -- higher and higher -- until the whole universe seems to spread out before our vision. For miles and miles beyond is one vast park of vivid green framed by the Continental Divide, with Evans, James, and Neva mountains and the Arapahoe [Arapaho] Peaks extending far above the rest of the range, always snow-capped, usually clothed in fleecy clouds, and making one feel that after all we are but pigmies in the great scheme of nature."

Boulder Canyon in the 1930s. Courtesy Daily Camera.

FOR FURTHER READING

Abele, Deborah Edge. *Metal Mining and Tourist Era Resources of Boulder County, National Register of Historic Places Multiple Property Listing.* Denver: Colorado Historical Society, 1989.

Bailey, Delores S., *God's Country U.S.A., Wallstreet, Colorado.* Fort Collins: Robinson Press, 1982.

Balsley, Robert. *Early Gold Hill.* Boulder: Robert Balsley, 1971.

Bancroft, Caroline. *Gulch of Gold, A History of Central City, Colorado.* Denver: Sage Books, 1958.

Becker, Isabel M. *Nederland, A Trip to Cloudland.* Denver: Scott Becker Press, 1989.

Bird, Isabella. *A Lady's Life in the Rocky Mountains.* Norman: University of Oklahoma Press, 1960.

Bixby, A., *"History of Boulder County,"* in *History of Clear Creek and Boulder Valleys.* Chicago: O. L. Baskin & Co., 1880.

Bollinger, Edward T., and Frederick Bauer. *The Moffat Road.* Denver: Sage Books, 1962.

Boulder County Metal Mining Association. *Mining in Boulder County, Colorado.* Boulder: Boulder County Metal Mining Association, 1919.

Boulder County Parks and Open Space. *Exploring Boulder County.* Boulder: Boulder County Parks and Open Space Department, 1988.

Brown, Robert L. *Central City and Gilpin County, Then and Now.* Caldwell: Caxton Printers, Ltd., 1994.

Buchanan, John W., and Doris G. Buchanan. *The Story of Ghost Town Caribou.* Boulder: Boulder Publishing, Inc., 1957.

Cobb, Harrison S. *Prospecting Our Past: Gold, Silver, and Tungsten Mills of Boulder County.* Boulder: Book Lode, 1988.

Crossen, Forest. *Boulder By-Ways, A Guidebook of Recommended Auto Tours In and Around Boulder.* Boulder: Boulder Savings and Loan Association, 1959.

Crossen, Forest. *The Switzerland Trail of America.* Boulder: Pruett Publishing, 1962.

Deno, William R. *Body and Soul, Architectural Style at the University of Colorado at Boulder.* Boulder: Regents of the University of Colorado, 1994.

Dever, Crete Childers. *Meeker Park and the Dever Family.* Meeker Park: privately published, 1970.

Dyni, Anne Quinby. *Back to the Basics, The Frontier Schools of Boulder County, 1860-1960.* Boulder: Book Lode, 1991.

Ellis, Jr., Russell. *Boulder, Colorado, Home of the Switzerland Trail.* Boulder: Boulder Motel Association, ca. mid-1960s.

Eson, Theo. *A Tale of Two Towns.* Nederland: Windmill Books & Gifts, 1986.

Foscue, Edwin J., and Louis O. Quam. *Estes Park, Resort in the Rockies.* Dallas: University Press in Dallas, 1949.

Galey, Mary. *Grand Assembly, The Story of Life at the Colorado Chautauqua.* Boulder: First Flatiron Press, 1981.

Howard, June Peterson. *Stories of Sunshine, Life in a Mining Camp.* Longmont: Book Lode, 1994.

Jones, Forrest. *The Back-History of Sunshine As I Recollect It.* Boulder: privately published, 1983.

Kemp, Donald C. *Colorado's Little Kingdom.* Golden: Sage Books, 1949.

Kemp, Donald C., and John R. Langley. *Happy Valley, A Promoter's Paradise, Being an Historic Sketch of Eldora, Colorado and Its Environs.* Denver: Smith-Brooks Printing Company, 1945.

Kemp, Donald C. *Silver, Gold and Black Iron, A Story of the Grand Island Mining District of Boulder County, Colorado.* Denver: Sage Books, 1960.

Knowlton, Lorna. *Weaving Mountain Memories, Recollections of the Allenspark Area.* Estes Park: Estes Park Historical Museum, 1989.

Lyons Historical Society. *Lyons and Surrounding Area.* Lyons: Lyons Centennial-Bicentennial Committee, 1977.

Meier, Thomas J. *Ed Tangen, The Pictureman, A Photographic History of the Boulder Region, Early Twentieth Century.* Boulder: Boulder Creek Press, 1994.

Messinger, Jean Goodwin, and Mary Jane Massey Rust. *Faith in High Places, Historic Country Churches of Colorado.* Boulder: Roberts Rinehart Publishers, 1995.

Montgomery, Mabel. *A Story of Gold Hill, Seventy-odd Years In the Heart of the Rockies.* Boulder: Book Lode (reprint by), 1987.

Parsons, Eugene. *A Guidebook to Colorado.* Boston: Little Brown & Company, 1911.

Pettem, Silvia. *Boulder: Evolution of a City.* Niwot: University Press of Colorado, 1994.

Pettem, Silvia. *Excursions From Peak to Peak Beginning in Boulder.* Boulder: Book Lode, 1987.

Pettem, Silvia. *Guide to Historic Western Boulder County.* Evergreen: Cordillera Press, 1989.

Pettem, Silvia. *Red Rocks to Riches, Gold Mining in Boulder County Then and Now.* Boulder: Stonehenge, 1980.

Pettem, Silvia. *The Peaceful Valley Story, Fulfillment of a Dream.* Boulder: Book Lode, 1994.

Rollins Pass Restoration Association. *The Moffat Road, A Self-guided Auto Tour.* Longmont: Rollins Pass Restoration Association (reprint by), 1996.

Sanford, Mollie Dorsey. *Mollie, The Journal of Mollie Dorsey Sanford in Nebraska & Colorado Territories, 1857-1866.* Lincoln: University of Nebraska Press, 1959.

Schoolland, J. B. *Boulder Then and Now.* Boulder: Pruett Press, 1967.

Smith, Duane A. *Silver Saga, The Story of Caribou, Colorado.* Boulder: Pruett Press, 1974.

Smith, Phyllis. *A Look at Boulder From Settlement to City.* Boulder: Pruett Press, 1981.

Tripp, Betty J., *The Pioneers of Caribou, A Silver Ghost Town.* Detroit: Betty J. Tripp, 1996.

Weaver, Frank. *"That Beautiful Valley," E. S. Lyon: A Man with a Dream.* Lyons: New Lyons Recorder, 1978.

Weiss, Manuel. *Boulder County Historical Site Survey.* Denver: Colorado Historical Society, 1981.

Yore, Clem, *Colorado, Rocky Mountain National (Estes) Park.* Chicago: Burlington Railroad Company, 1930.

INDEX

Historic buildings and districts (other than hotels, resorts, and railroads):
    Boulder Downtown Historic District, 109.
    Bunce School, 93-94.
    Camp Saint Milo, 97-98.
    Carnegie Library, 109.
    Central City / Black Hawk Historic District, 38.
    Chautauqua Park, 110-111.
    Eldora Historic District, 46, 51.
    Enos Mills homestead cabin, 101-102.
    Gold Hill Historic District, 76-77.
    Lace House, 39.
    Little Church in the Pines, 7.
    Lyons Railroad Depot, 13, 106-107.
    Lyons Sandstone Buildings, 107.
    Lyons School, 107.
    Mapleton Hill Historic District, 109.
    Norlin Quadrangle Historic District, 109-110.
    Saint Catherine's Chapel. See Camp Saint Milo.
    Salina School, 6.
    Sunshine School, 77-78.
    Teller Opera House, 38.
    Ward Congregational (Community) Church, 81-84.
    Ward School, 79, 81.

Hotels and resorts (historic):
    Antlers Hotel, 58.
    Baldpate Inn, 102-103.
    Blue Bird Lodge, 74-75.
    C & N Hotel, 11.
    Columbia Hotel, 11, 82-83.
    Copeland Lake Lodge, 22, 96.
    Crystal Springs Lodge, 94.
    Dixie Lodge, 53.
    Double M Ranch (Trojan Ranch), 77.
    Elkhorn Lodge, 103.
    English Hotel, 103.
    Forest Inn Hotel, 91. See also, Peaceful Valley.
    Glacier View Lodge, 11.
    Gold Miner Hotel, 48, 51.
    Hetzer House Hotel, 56-57.
    Hewes-Kirkwood Inn, 22, 101.
    Hotel Boulderado, 31.
    Hotel McClancy, 81.
    Hotel Stanley, 13-14, 103.
    Lodge of the Pines, 11.
    Longs Peak Inn, 21-22, 101-102.
    Meeker Park Lodge, 96-97.
    Peaceful Valley, 1-2, 11, 15-17, 22, 25, 33-34, 90-93, 105.
    Pine Log Lodge, 53.
    Raymonds Hotel, 93.
    Sherman House Hotel, 62.
    Stage Stop Inn, 40.
    Stanley Hotel. See Hotel Stanley.
    Stapp's Lake Lodge, 10-11, 86.
    Teller House Hotel, 37.

The Columbines, 22, 101.
Utica Hotel, 11.
Wentworth Hotel. See Blue Bird Lodge.
Wild Basin Lodge, 96. See also, Copeland Lake Lodge.
Will's Resort (Presbyterian Highlands Ranch), 94.

Museums:
- Boulder Museum of History, 109.
- Eagle Plume's, 98.
- Estes Park Historical Museum, 104.
- Redstone Museum, 107.
- University of Colorado Heritage Center, 110.

Natural sites:
- Arapaho Glacier, 25-32, 50-51, 54.
- Boulder Falls, 114-115, 117.
- Brainard Lake, 87-89, 105-106.
- Castle Rock, 117.
- Copeland Lake, 93, 95.
- Indian Peaks Wilderness, 20, 25, 87-88, 105.
- Longs Peak, 13, 93, 98-99, 101.
- Mount Meeker, 95.
- Perfect Tree, 116-117.
- Red Rock Lake, 89.
- Rocky Mountain National Park, 1, 19, 20-21, 23, 25, 29-30, 34, 86, 96, 98, 101-102, 104.
- Sheep's Head Rock, 100.
- Wild Basin, 95-96.
- Yoo-Hoo Point, 17.

People:
- Adams, Governor Alva, 53, 80.
- Alexander, Addie, 98.
- Allen, Alonzo N., 93.

Bierstadt, Albert, 103.
Bird, Isabella, 98-99.
Breed, A. D., 56.
Brown, Nathan W. and Caroline, 55.
Byers, William N., 98.
Darrow, Clarence, 74.
Davis, Herndon, 38.
Dickinson, Anna, 98.
Dunraven, Lord, 103.
Eagle Plume, Charles, 98.
Estes, Joel, 103.
Fair, Fred, 26-27, 29, 31, 117.
Field, Eugene, 74.
Fine, Eben G., 27, 108.
Grant, President Ulysses S., 37.
Gunn, Old Man, 98.
Hill, Nathaniel P., 37.
Jackson, Helen Hunt, 111.
James, W. E., 103.
Kemp, John H., 47.
Lindbergh, Charles, 29.
Long, Major Stephen H., 98.
Lyon, Edward S., 107.
Marshall, R. B., 19, 21, 30.
Meyring, Henry, 74.
Mills, Enos, 21, 27, 101-102.
Moffat, David Halliday, 41-44.
Powell, Major John Wesley, 98.
Rollins, John Quincy Adams, 40-42.
Saint Vrain, Ceran, 106.
Stanley, F. E., 13.

Stanley, F. O., 13-14, 103, 107.
Tabor, Horace and Baby Doe, 38, 79-80.
Teller, Senator Henry M., 38.
Verne, Jules, 98.
Railroads:
    Burlington, 27.
    Colorado & Northwestern, 8, 10, 49, 59, 66-67, 70. See also, Switzerland Trail.
    Colorado Central, 37.
    Denver & Interurban, 29.
    Denver & Rio Grande (Western), 44. See also, Denver, Northwestern & Pacific (Moffat Road).
    Denver & Salt Lake, 44. See also, Denver, Northwestern & Pacific (Moffat Road).
    Denver, Boulder & Western, 21, 70. See also, Switzerland Trail.
    Denver, Northwestern & Pacific (Moffat Road), 1, 11-12, 41-45, 66.
    Denver, Utah & Pacific, 106.
    Greeley, Salt Lake & Pacific, 8-9, 65. See also, Switzerland Trail.
    Moffat Road (see Denver, Northwestern & Pacific Railway).
    Stone Mountain, 108.
    Switzerland Trail (of America), 1, 8-9, 12, 21-22, 65-71, 78-79, 86, 105, 114.
Roads (other than Peak to Peak Highway):
    Boulder Canyon (Canon), 2-4, 29, 31, 55, 57, 59, 105, 108, 111-114, 117, 119.
    Fall River Road, 23, 104.
    Highline/Skyline Drive, 15-16, 33, 93.
    Left Hand Canyon, 4, 22, 79, 108.

Rollins Pass, 12, 41-45.
South Saint Vrain Canyon, 16, 93, 100, 105-106, 111.
Trail Ridge Road, 34, 104.

Towns, townsites, and railroad stops:
Allenspark (Allen's Park), 1-2, 4, 16, 22, 93-95, 103.
Black Hawk, 1-5, 36-39, 56-57, 60, 79.
Camp Frances, 67, 85.
Cardinal, 60, 64, 70.
Caribou, 4-5, 37, 54, 56-64, 105, 111.
Central City, 1, 4, 10, 37-38, 48, 57, 64, 103.
Corona, 12, 43, 45.
Eldora, 1, 9-10, 19, 31, 47-54, 58-59, 68.
Estes Park, 1-2, 13-16, 19, 21-22, 86, 90, 93, 101-104.
Ferncliff, 34, 93, 95.
Glacier Lake, 10, 69-71.
Gold Hill, 1, 3, 4, 9, 37, 48, 66, 71-78, 105.
Gold Hill station, 66, 71, 78.
Gresham, 16.
Happy Valley. See Eldora.
Jamestown, 11, 16.
Lake Eldora area, 47, 52-54.
Lyons, 1-2, 13, 93, 104-108.
Magnolia, 57, 111, 114.
Meeker Park, 2, 34, 93, 96-97.
Mont Alto, 9, 66-67, 69, 71.
Nederland, 1-2, 4-5, 15, 21-22, 25, 33-34, 37, 54-60, 64, 71, 78-79, 105, 111, 118.
Peaceful Valley. See Hotels and resorts (historic), Peaceful Valley.
Pennsylvania (Penn) Gulch, 4, 65. See also, Sunset.
Peterson Lake (Lake Ha Ha Tonka). See Lake Eldora area.

Puzzler, 4, 22.
Quigleyville, 11.
Raymond, 16, 33, 93.
Rollinsville, 1, 2, 4, 12, 37, 40-45.
Salina, 5-6, 74.
Sugarloaf station, 71.
Sulphide Flats, 47, 52, 54, 59, 69.
Sunnyside, 4.
Sunset, 8-9, 65-69, 71, 79. See also, Pennsylvania Gulch.
Sunshine, 5, 77-78.
Tolland, 45.
Wallstreet, 5.
Ward, 1-5, 8-11, 13, 15, 19, 21-22, 25, 33-34, 37, 48, 56, 65-68, 70-71, 79-86, 89-90, 92, 101, 105, 108.
Wildcat Gulch. See Peaceful Valley.